IRREVOCABLE

POEMS AND MEDITATIONS TO HOLD IT ALL

WHOLENESS

OTHER WORKS

Kyle Leia (Elden) Heyesen
Grace Intoxicated: A Collection of Poems
Driftwood Press 2012

Sarah Brokke
Portrait of an Artist
Holy Cow! Press 2016

Illustrated by Sarah Brokke
Common Thirst by Gary Boelhower
Beavers Pond Press 2020

IRREVOCABLE

POEMS AND MEDITATIONS TO HOLD IT ALL

WHOLENESS

POEMS BY KYLE LEIA | PAINTINGS BY SARAH BROKKE

DRIFTWOOD PRESS, DULUTH, MN

Book design: Deb Davidsavor
Cover image: Sarah Brokke *To Hold It All* 36″ x 48″, Oil on Canvas, 2022
Printed locally at Pro-Print in Duluth, MN

ISBN: 979-8-9998983-0-2

DEDICATION

For my Beloveds – Jon Heyesen and Stella Molina ~ Kyle Leia

For my Mother, who has always held it all for me ~ Sarah Brokke

TABLE OF CONTENTS

PROLOGUE

Irrevocable Wholeness: Poems and Meditations to Hold it All is a collection of poems and meditations in conversation with visual art. This offering provides unique pathways to support more skillfully holding space for our lives exactly as they are. It is first and foremost a reminder that we are all irrevocably whole. When we realize the spaciousness of our being and the divine compass embedded in our own hearts, we begin to sense that we are large enough to hold our pain instead of being decimated by it. We are made for this. We begin to open ourselves to the limitless healing capacity that is our birthright. To hold it all does not mean that the inevitable suffering of life continuously heaps on and becomes heavier daily. It is a contemplative journey of exploration within. It is a reconnection with our truest, wisest Self calibrating with our highest values and life's purpose. It is a reclamation of our wholeness. It is learning to recognize our true capacity and how to build inner- and outer-resources. It is our innate connection to the divine, the spark within that gives us life. It is knowing how to release, let go, move through, alchemize, and transform. To hold it all is our magic, our purpose, and our unique manifestation here on earth. It is our heartstrings to joy, pleasure, and aliveness.

NOTE FROM THE POET

I've made it a practice to walk through the world open to receive guidance, insights, and illuminations. I have been utterly gobsmacked, broken open, and more able to get through difficulties of life with the poetry that has been given to me. It is a gift that I do not own, it comes to me and through me, yet belongs to us all. The earth speaks, nature is a teacher, the luminosity of the moon magical, and the gentle floating of a fat bumble bee over red clovers, somehow divine. All whisper ancient wisdom, instructions on how to live wholly. Sarah had a dream about this collaboration, listened intently, reached out to me and invited me in. Every cell in my body lit up with, "Yes!" I'm forever grateful to her. The culmination of many years of poetry and meditations suddenly came into focus for this purpose. Her paintings and my poems revealed from our collective unconscious, through different mediums, became a beautiful guide for humanity.

NOTE FROM THE PAINTER

The images in this collection represent a portion of the body of work I've undertaken over the past eight years. Originating in dreams and what I have begun to believe are echoes of distant once-lived memories, this work navigates the space between the external world and our internal lives. I visually transcribe water as it transforms into roots, which, in turn become veins; a mirror of nature and the cosmos found within our physical bodies. Through painting contemporary mythologies on canvas, I am testing the boundaries of finding the sacred in the secular, visioning towards the future. I believe it is imperative to develop a path through our present and beyond; making the liminal tangible.

Many of the pieces are cropped from their original format, and as with Kyle's work, exist as artworks on their own. Some of the work has inspired the other; paintings originated from poems, and poems inspired by paintings. Together, Kyle and I have created a conversation between our work; a third, collaborative entity, manifested in this book and the compendium oracle cards, with the intent to create reflective and healing spaces. It was truly a gift to collaborate on this project, and it is our hope that this is a gift that continues to give to you.

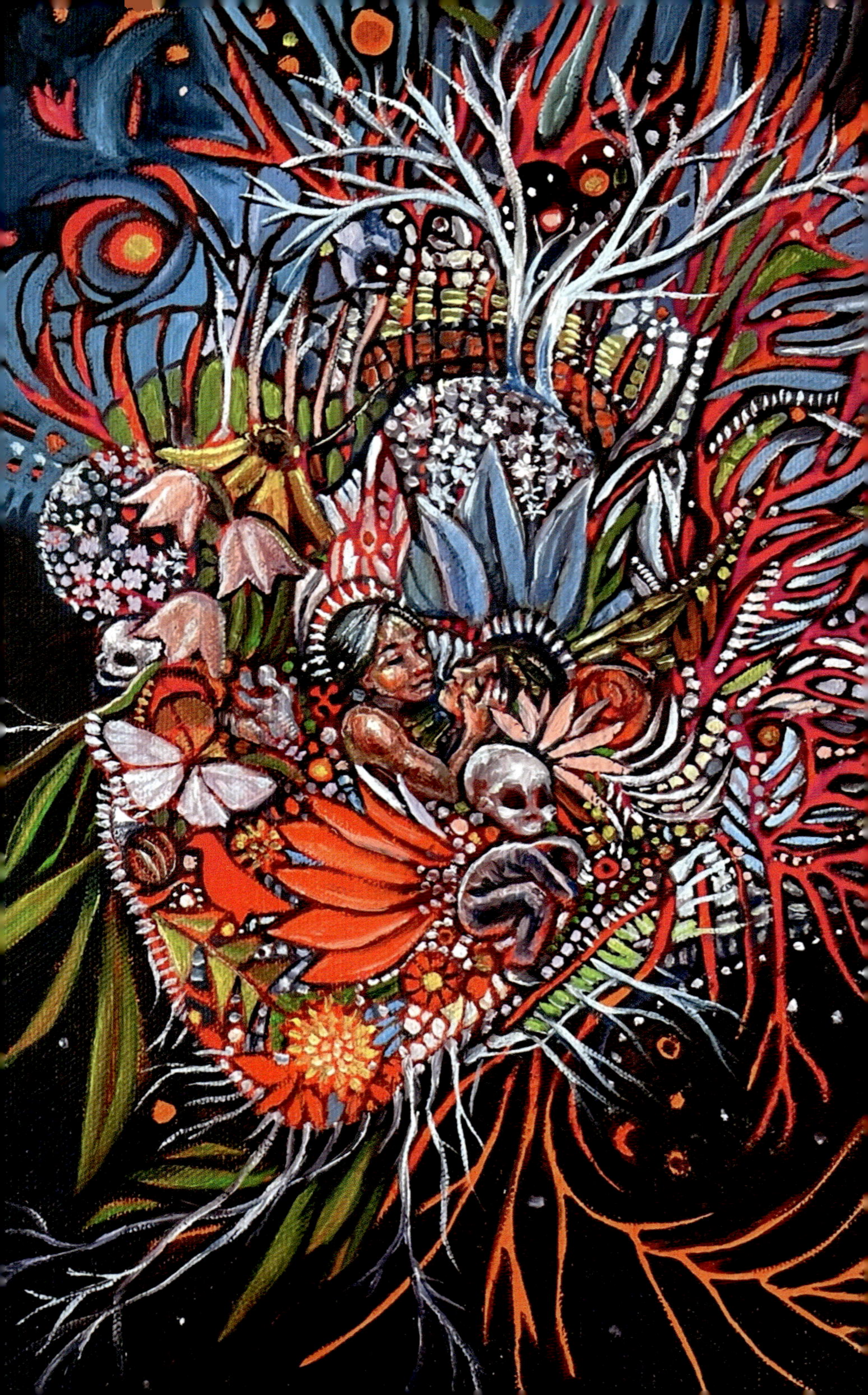

Awaken

When you are called to awaken
sometimes, sometimes
you turn your gaze away.

Dawn breaks, daylight fills your room
opens possibility, unfurls promise
the birds sing and sing
you begin to stir
but the sun strains your eyes
you shut the windows
draw the shades, pull the covers
over your head, go back to sleep.

What if today were different?
What if this is the moment to awaken?
What if you don't delay joy?
Like a child tearing into a present,
in fury and gladness
the gift of their desire shining
and revealed
so much is possible
tear into your precious life.

Awaken
press play
the arrow pointing in the direction forward
break silence
the click, the hum, the music of joy
coming in on surround sound.
Find yourself dancing everywhere,
even on ice covered sidewalks
in twenty-five below wind-chill
the music of joy IS coming in
on surround sound.

AFFIRMATION

I listen to the continual call to awaken
opening to my unique potential, my sacred purpose
I tune-in to the music of joy coming in on surround sound
and dance my heart out, a revolutionary refusal to delay delight

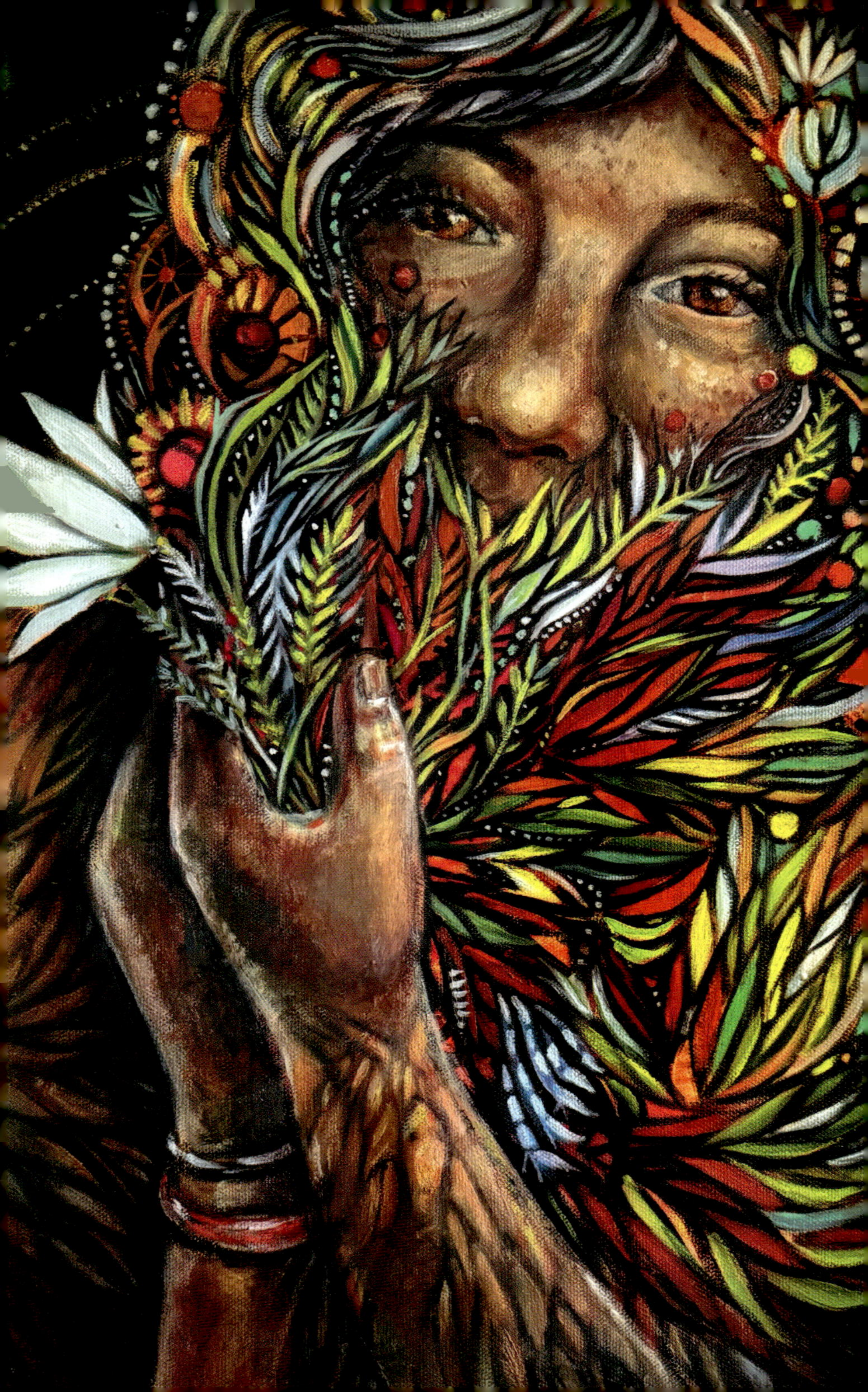

An Ending, a Beginning

I love how the trees
leave a mess of their leaves
no apologies
aflame with red and yellow
burning with their letting go
not afraid
shaking, falling, loosening
a slow drift down
or wind whipped
until bare
and they are not shivering
no matter the pain
all things eventually wane
they are ready
an ending, a beginning

AFFIRMATION

I release my grasp for control as I move through inevitable cycles of life
I invite the messiness and pain of change with greater ease
I am like the trees and tap into my strength and capacity to hold it all
I am ready for all the shifts, experiences, endings, and beginnings of life

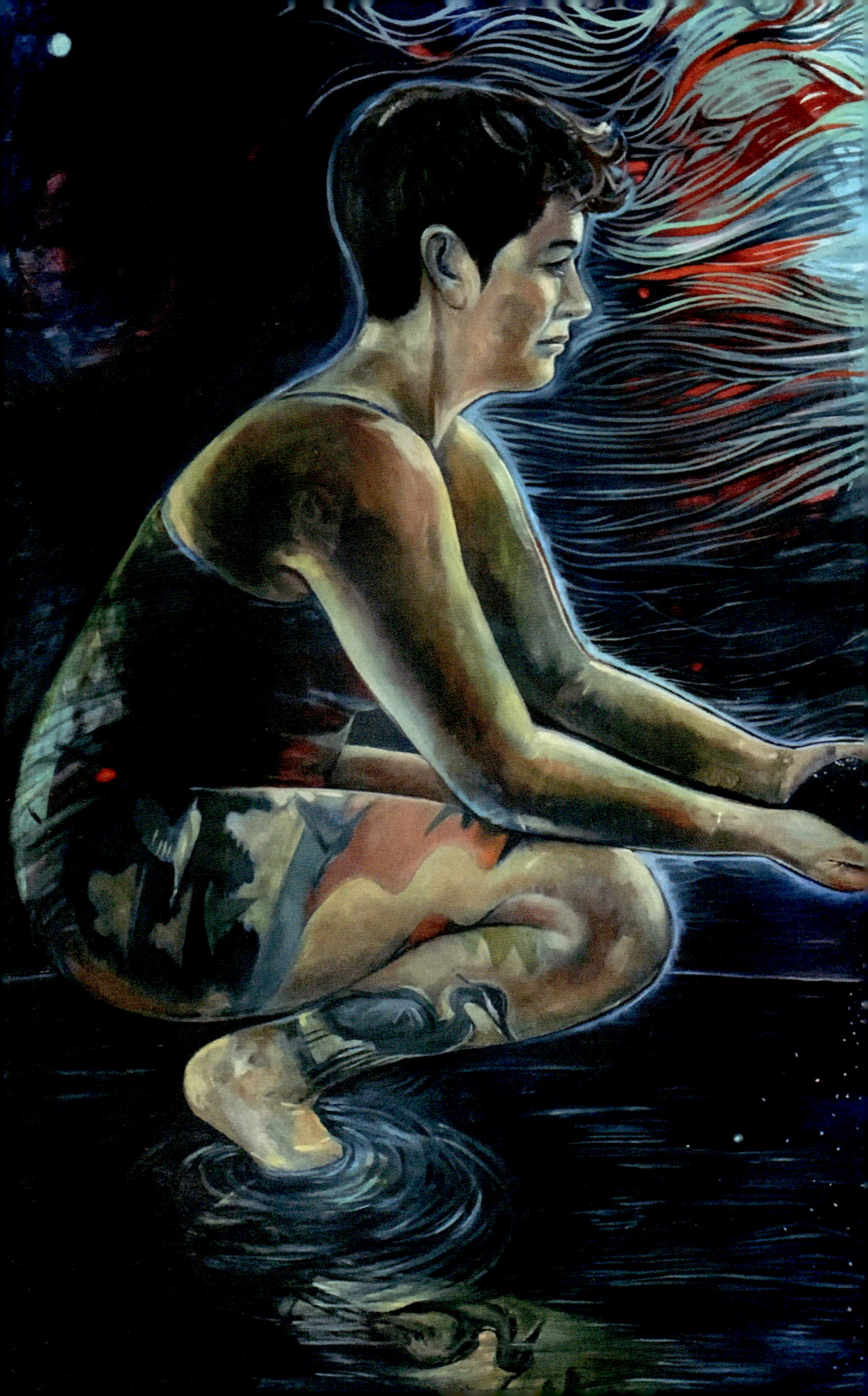

Beach Glass

When something shatters a
part of you, it never becomes
unshattered, does not return to the
shape it once was

Healing doesn't forget
the broken edges
the space
between what happened
and how it changed you forever

It moves like water
and holds the ground beneath
you like sand
as the pieces
tumble and stumble
around and forward

Until the sharp edges
soften against the movement
of time, forgiveness, and the fierce
waves of loving yourself

Eventually becoming beautiful
emerald and turquoise jewels
shining on the
shoreline of your being

AFFIRMATION

I open myself to the natural elements of healing
the sharp edges of my wounds soften like beach glass

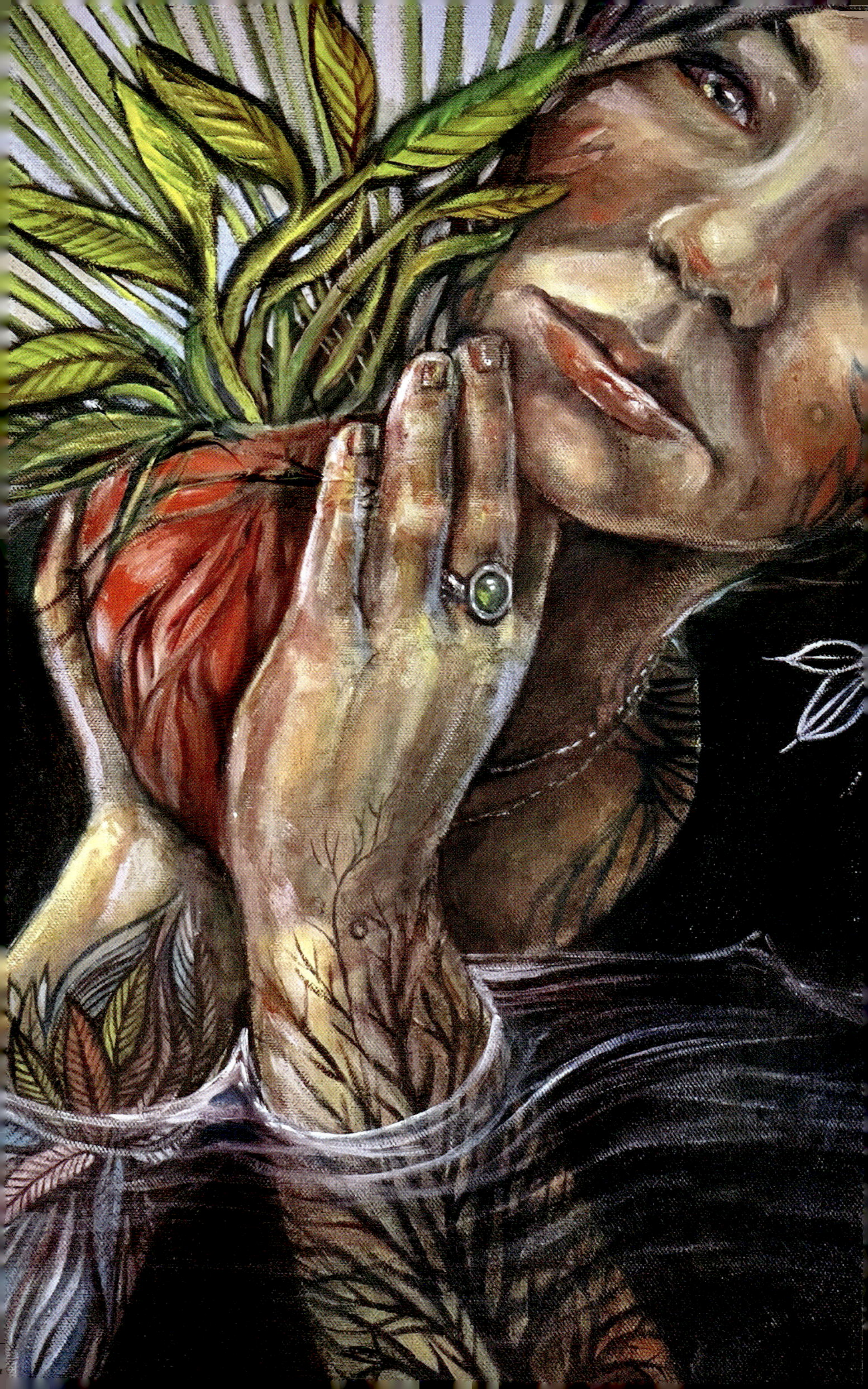

Beingness

After winter
the first nicest day
I lay on my deck
soaking in the sun medicine

Sometimes it is this simple
worries quiet, strain settles

Beingness begins

I am just
here

And it is miraculous (extraordinary)
how the light of the sun is invisible but warm
and somehow transfers vitamin D
a necessary nutrient, to me

I take it in and know how the trees, too
that give me air to breathe
are also fed in this way
the threads between us
all of us, all of us
delicately strung together

This thrumming Life Force
that builds our beating hearts

AFFIRMATION

I rest in my Beingness
Just this. Here. Now.
I tune in to the thrumming Life Force
the rhythmic heartbeat of all creation

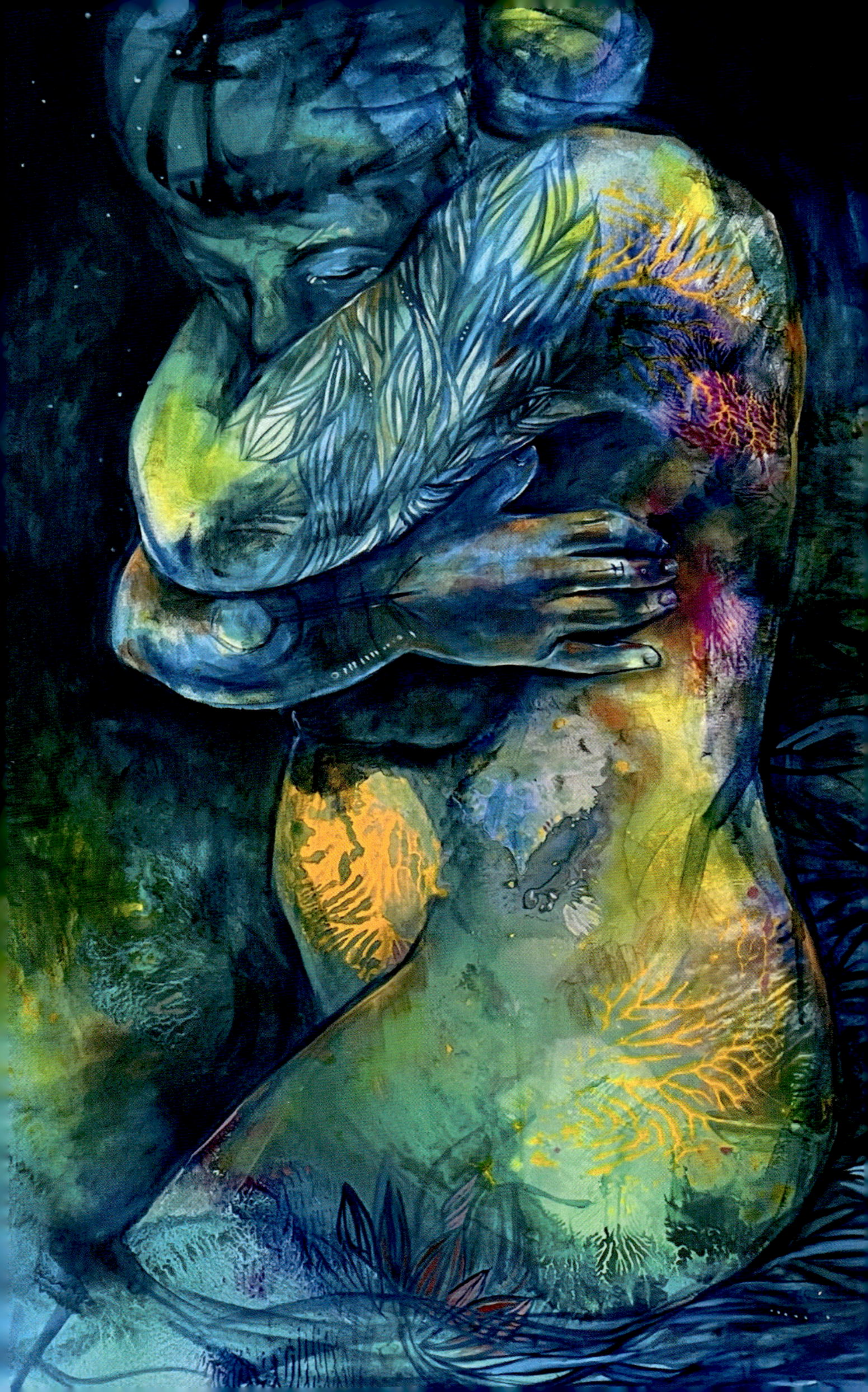

Beloved

You are divinely loved beyond reason
exactly as you are

You come from the source of Love
and are always held in that Love

You are Love and Love is you

As a dog chases its own tail
you chase Love in circles
not realizing what you so desperately seek
already belongs to you

Instead be still
be
Beloved

AFFIRMATION

I am loved and lovable
I am Beloved

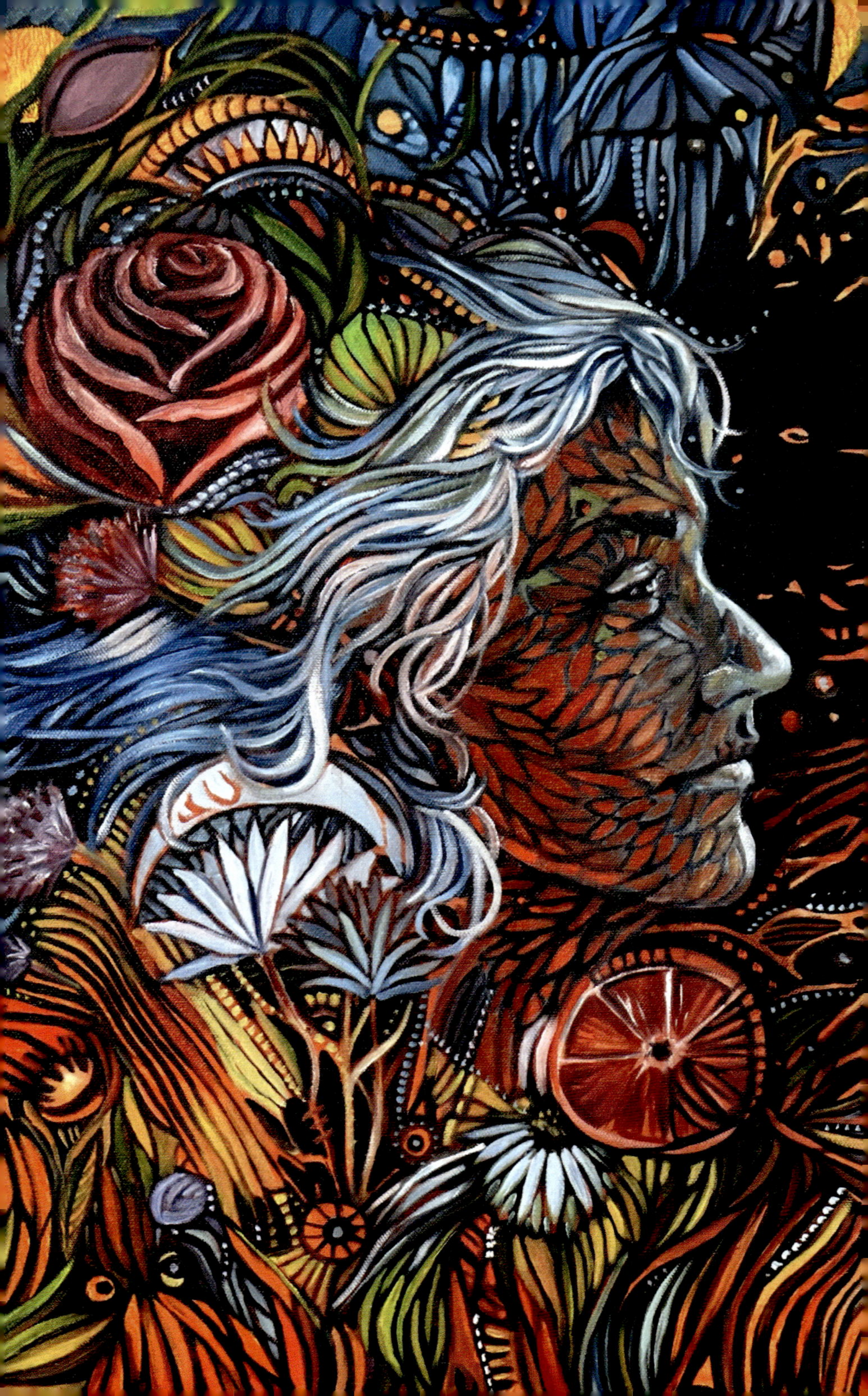

Bright Being

You looked into my eyes
saw the parts of me I couldn't

helped me find myself
lying in a pile of rocks

cruddy, rough edges all I could see
turned me over
said, "look at the beauty,
the strength, the worth!"
and all the layers, colors,
complexity, and heart shone through
like an agate
bright in the palm of your hand

AFFIRMATION

I see myself in my wholeness
I accept love from others who know me,
reflecting back my worthiness
I am lovely and lovable

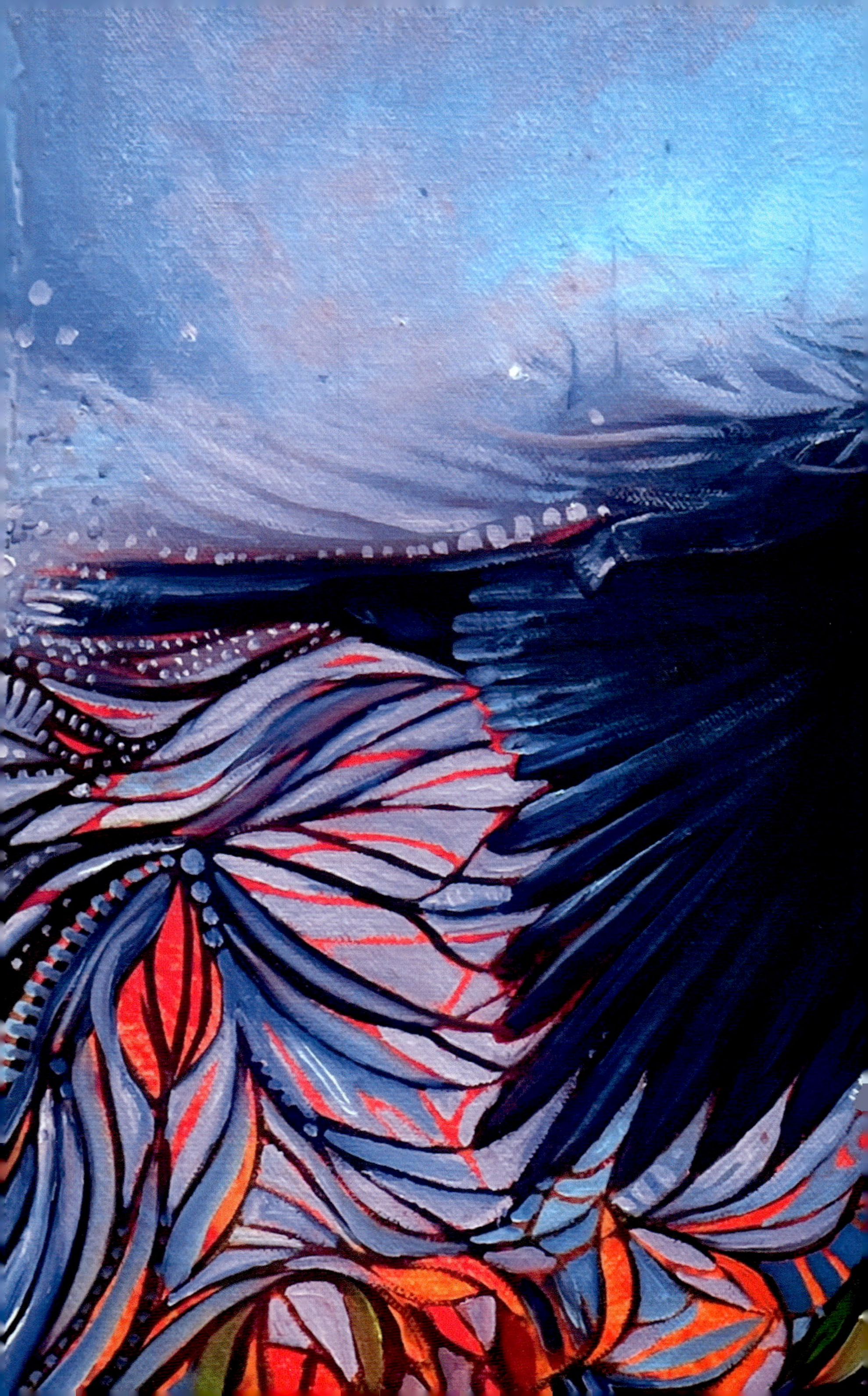

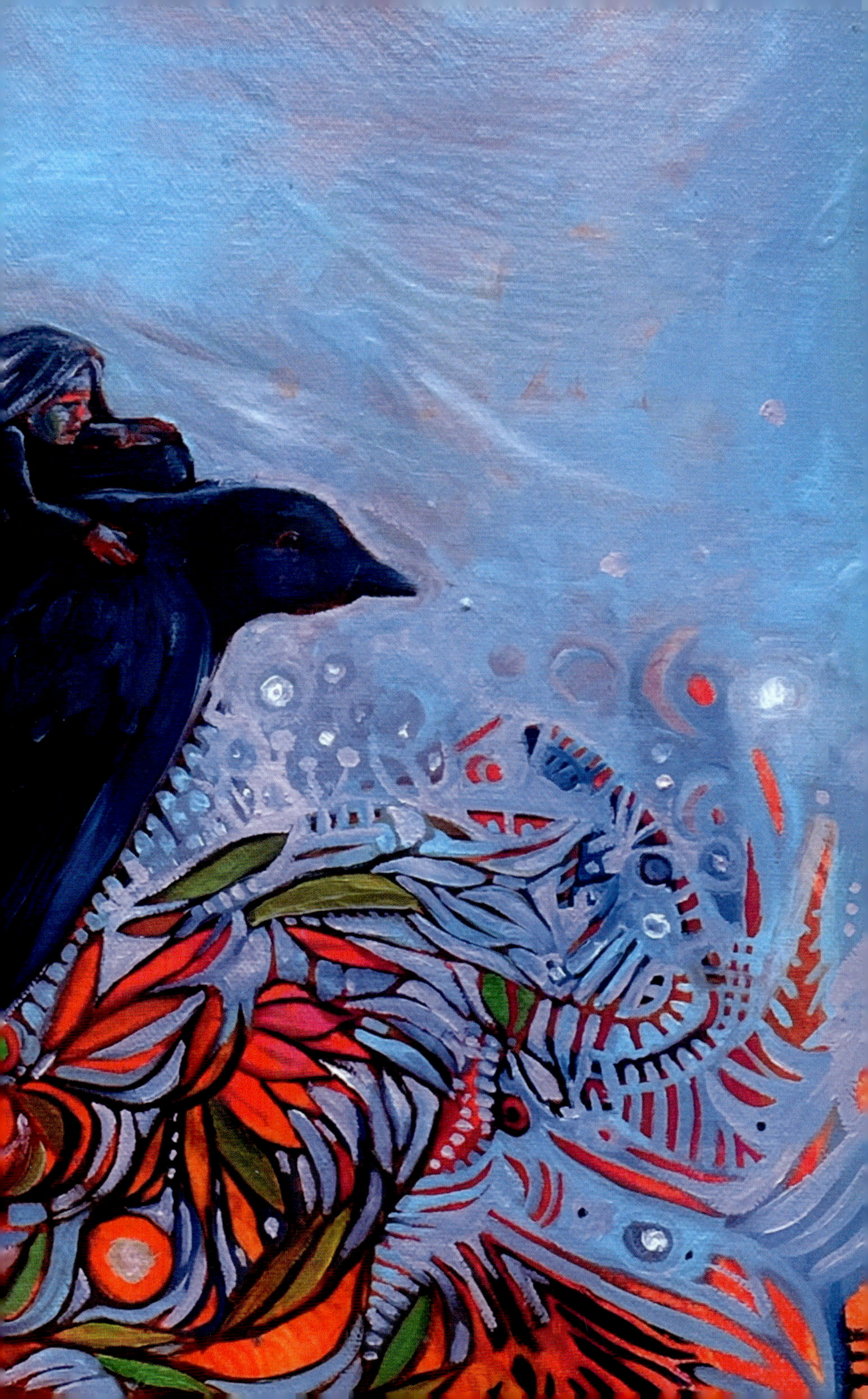

Carry Me

I've loosened my grip
from dreams that have died
hands grasp
want to hold what hurts
to prove it was true
"Here, can I show you?"

I'm meant to fly
and only I
hold keys to the cage
this bird wants to sing
has no broken wing
(no broken wing)
but still bangs
from within

I learned to let go
this breaking
broke me
open

Dissolved my desire
to undo the past
blame held
nearly choked me
a hard edged sugar cube
in my mouth
becomes liquid

Forgiveness is the sweetness
of swallowing truth
releases the pain
(releases the pain)
the love has changed
but love still remains
now this bird sweetly sings
rising up on great wings
carries me higher
(carries me higher)

AFFIRMATION

I rise above the difficulties
dissolve my desire to undo the past
release blame, transform pain
I am carried higher

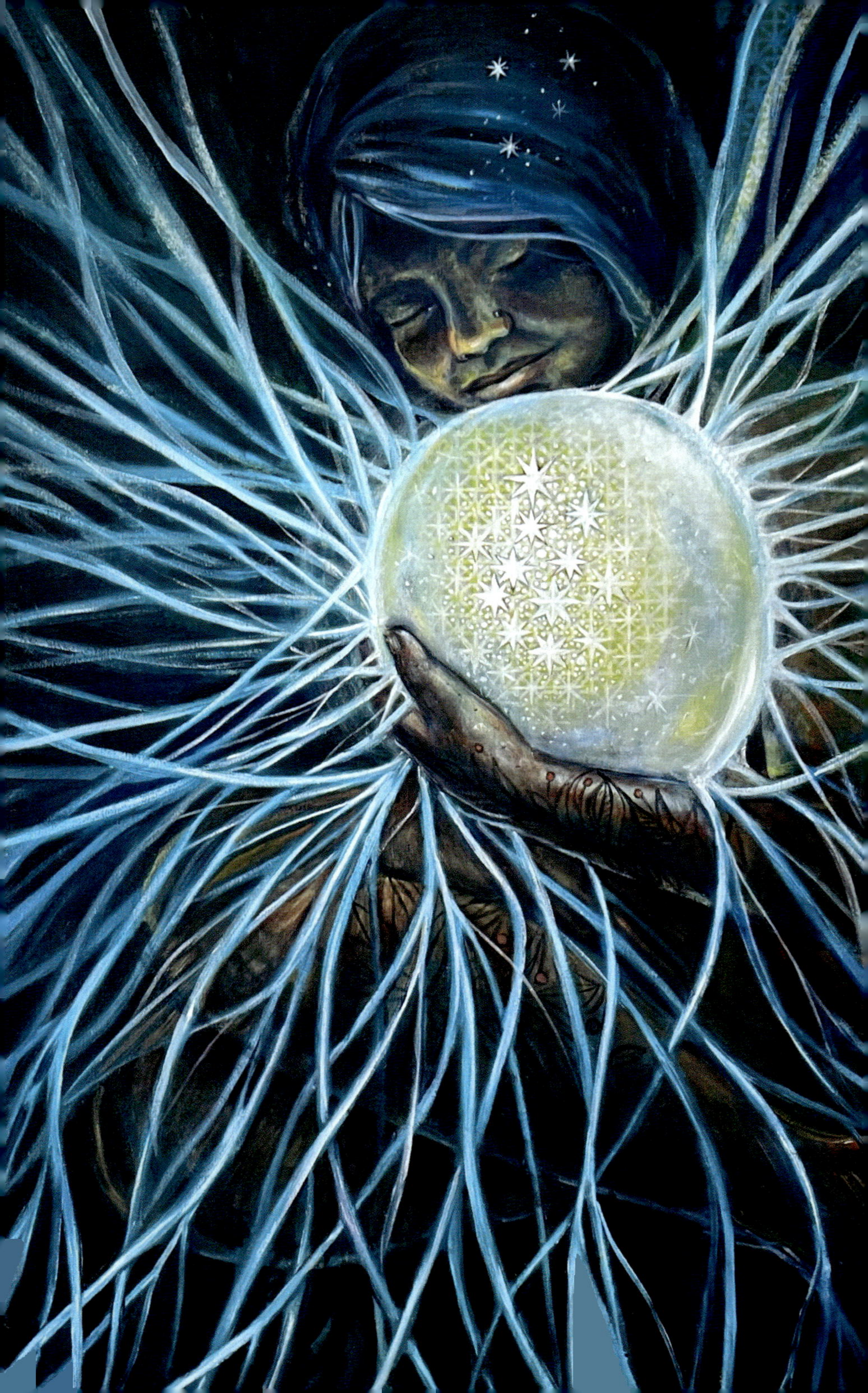

Constellations

Let the galaxies of worry spin

The stars of your days
burn tiny white flames

There is a vantage point
from where you can see
how the shape of
all your experiences
form constellations

From here, suddenly
it all makes wondrous sense

AFFIRMATION

I rest in the greater meaning of my life
and trust the unfolding story of my precious existence

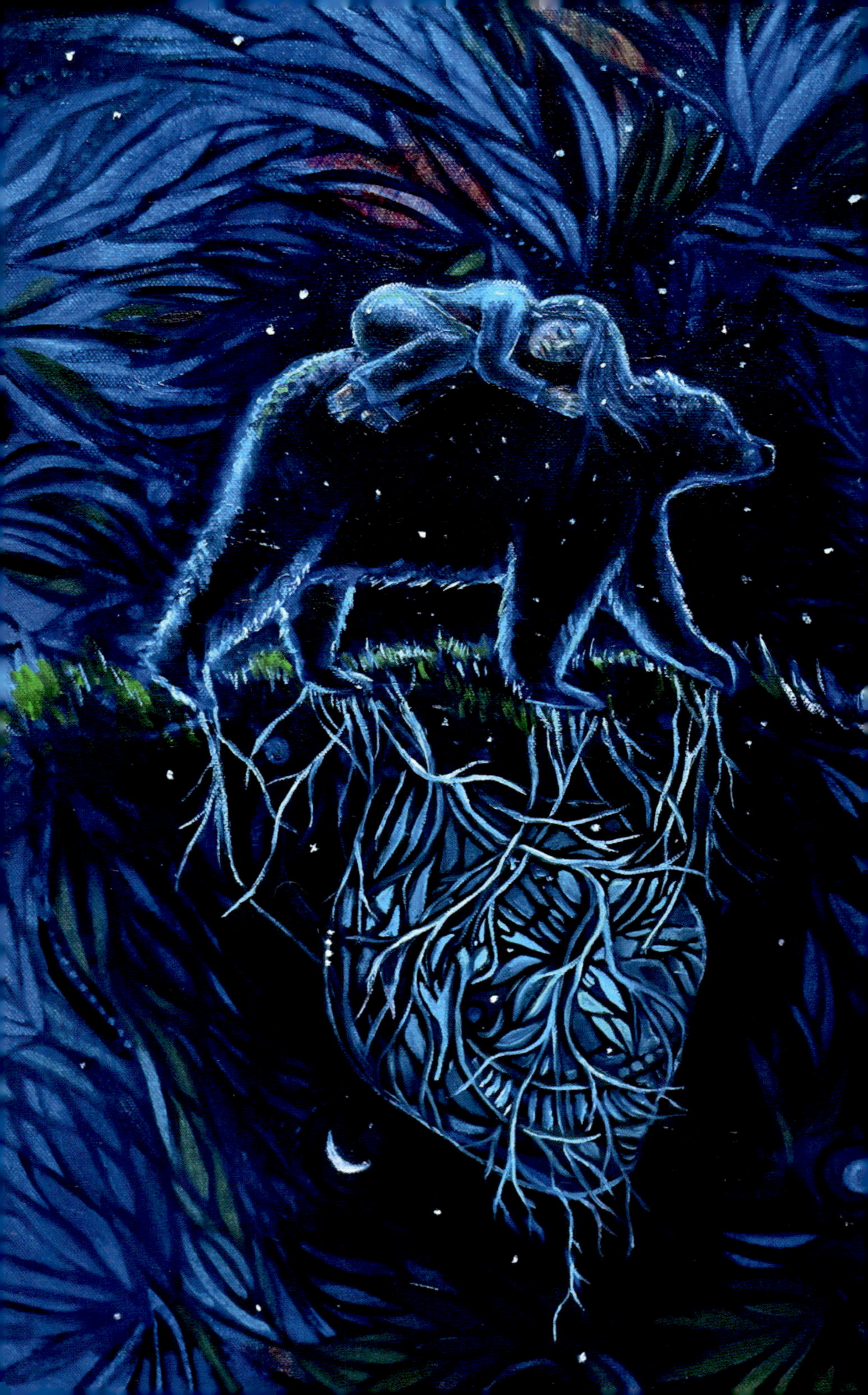

Deep Rest

How long have you carried the weight of the world on your shoulders
fueled by the adrenaline of your own resilience?
How much armor have you built up around yourself
inside your own beautiful body, this tightly spun tension
to survive the world?
How often have you pulled yourself up
been applauded, awarded, admired for your strength?
How many ways do you quiet the whispers of knowing
(momma bear spirit within, wise grandmother ancestors,
healers, heart of creation)
ignore the powerful ancient cry of deep rest?

You do not only have to be resilient.
You do not only need to survive.
You do not have to be strong all of the time.
You are enough just as you are.

May you lay your sweet head down for a while
return to the Mother of us all
be carried on her warm, strong back.
You are worthy of care. Allow yourself to be held.
Draw from this deep well of peace.
You deserve to be filled with this primal love.
Protected.
Your life depends on it.

This is the resistance.
This is the revolution.

AFFIRMATION

My deep rest is a radical act
I am held and protected by the Mother of us all
I draw from this deep well of peace
I am filled with primordial love

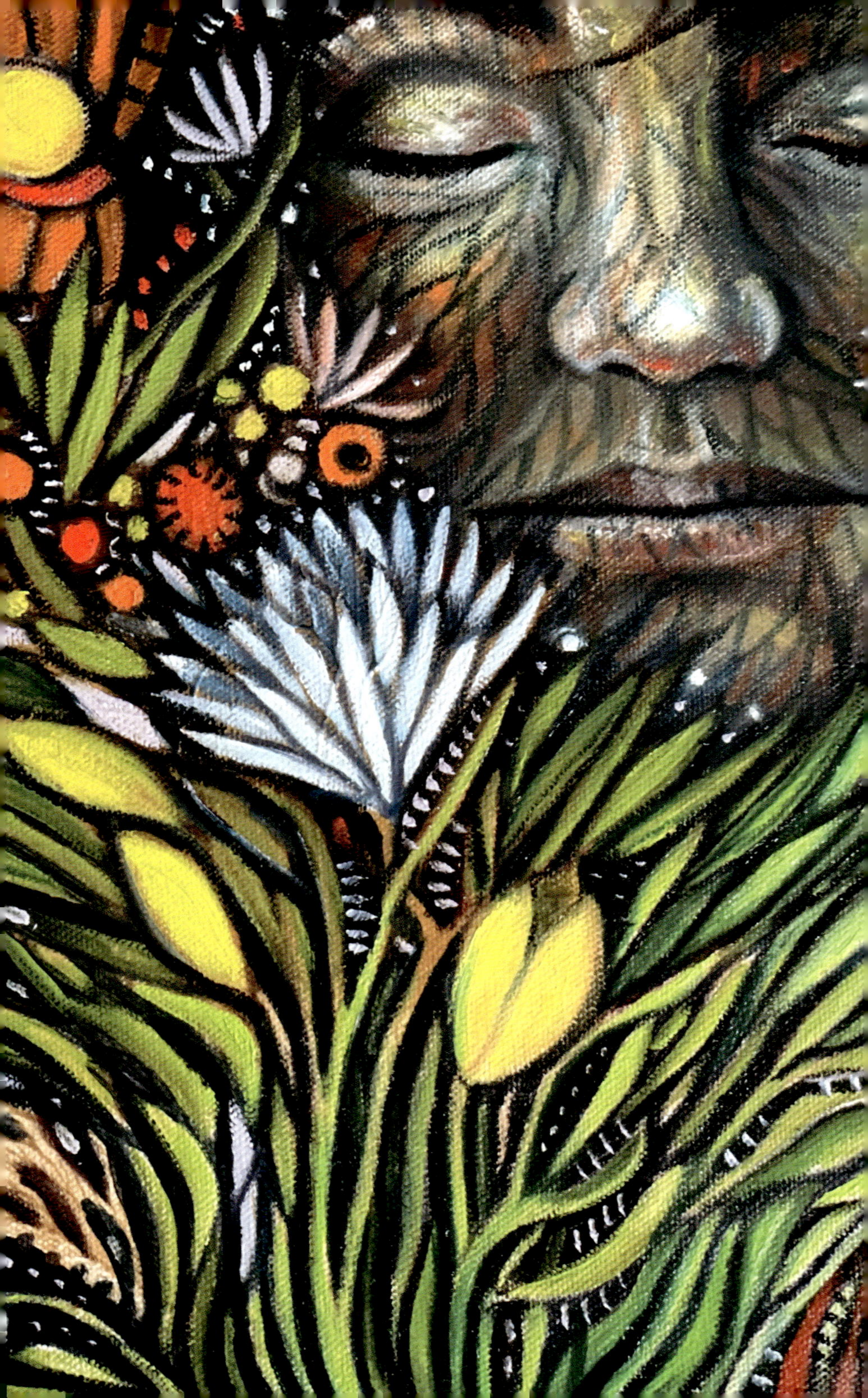

Devastating Beauty

We spend so much of our lives bracing, bracing
worried to death we hold our breath

Gather up this worry
like gold and red leaves in autumn
put them all in a leaf pile
jump into it with joy
(or rage or whatever is real for you in this moment)
throw them around like confetti
feel how they are dried up and crunchy
crumble in your hands and under your feet
hold no real weight
let yourself laugh as you
notice that the ground beneath holds you
and seasons continue to move forward regardless
because your fear is not a shield, there is no stopping life
so you may as well dance with it instead
and have fun whenever possible
and lay on your back and look up
at the endless blue sky with awe
through delicate designs made of bare tree branches
the crescent moon a translucent smudge
rare as a fingerprint in the afternoon sky
your breath, your body,
your tears, your rage,
your grief, your love,
your being
and know you are alive in all this
devastating beauty

AFFIRMATION

I recognize my fear is not a shield, I cannot stop life
I meet my worry with compassionate presence and lovingly tend to it
I turn my attention to my aliveness and choose to hold onto
the joy and beauty available to me even in difficulty

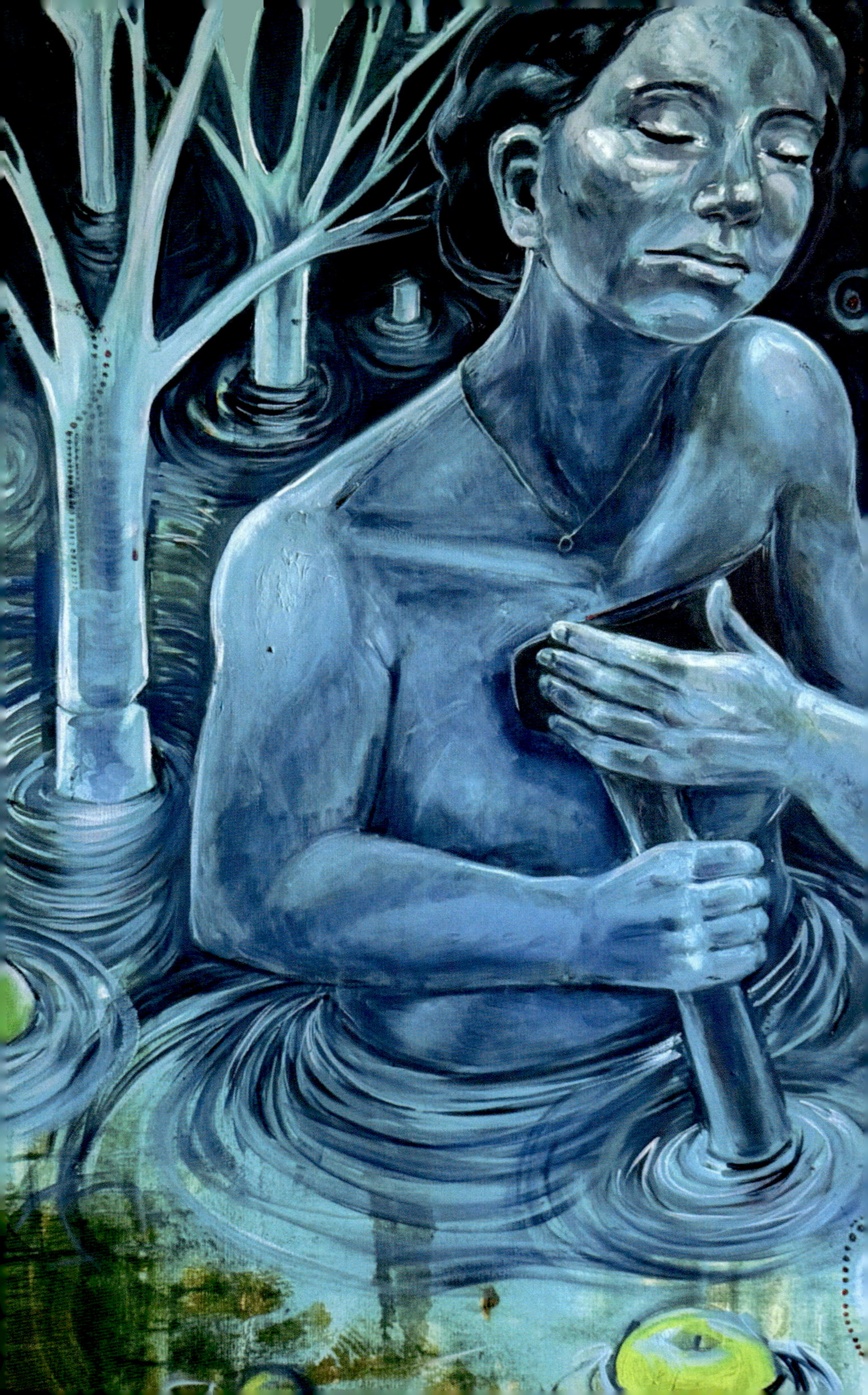

Eden

What if this world is not fully fallen
but being human has always been hard
and there was never a long-ago
faraway place
Eden that we are East of
but we are amidst and within it now
and have always been
((In the Garden))
the suffering, the sacred,
the profane, the divine
are all part of living
the Tree of Life
always within reach

What if the greatest sin
did not come from the snake
and the apple
but from not knowing
we are already here?

So push through
the flaming sword
flashing back and forth
to guard the way to the Tree
of the Knowledge of
Good and Evil
reclaim the red apple
make vats of golden juice
and drink up
this sweet knowing

AFFIRMATION

In each precious day throughout my life
I taste the sweetness of knowing both sacred and profane
I experience the ways we are In the Garden
and contribute to creating as much peace,
beauty, love, and kindness as is humanly possible

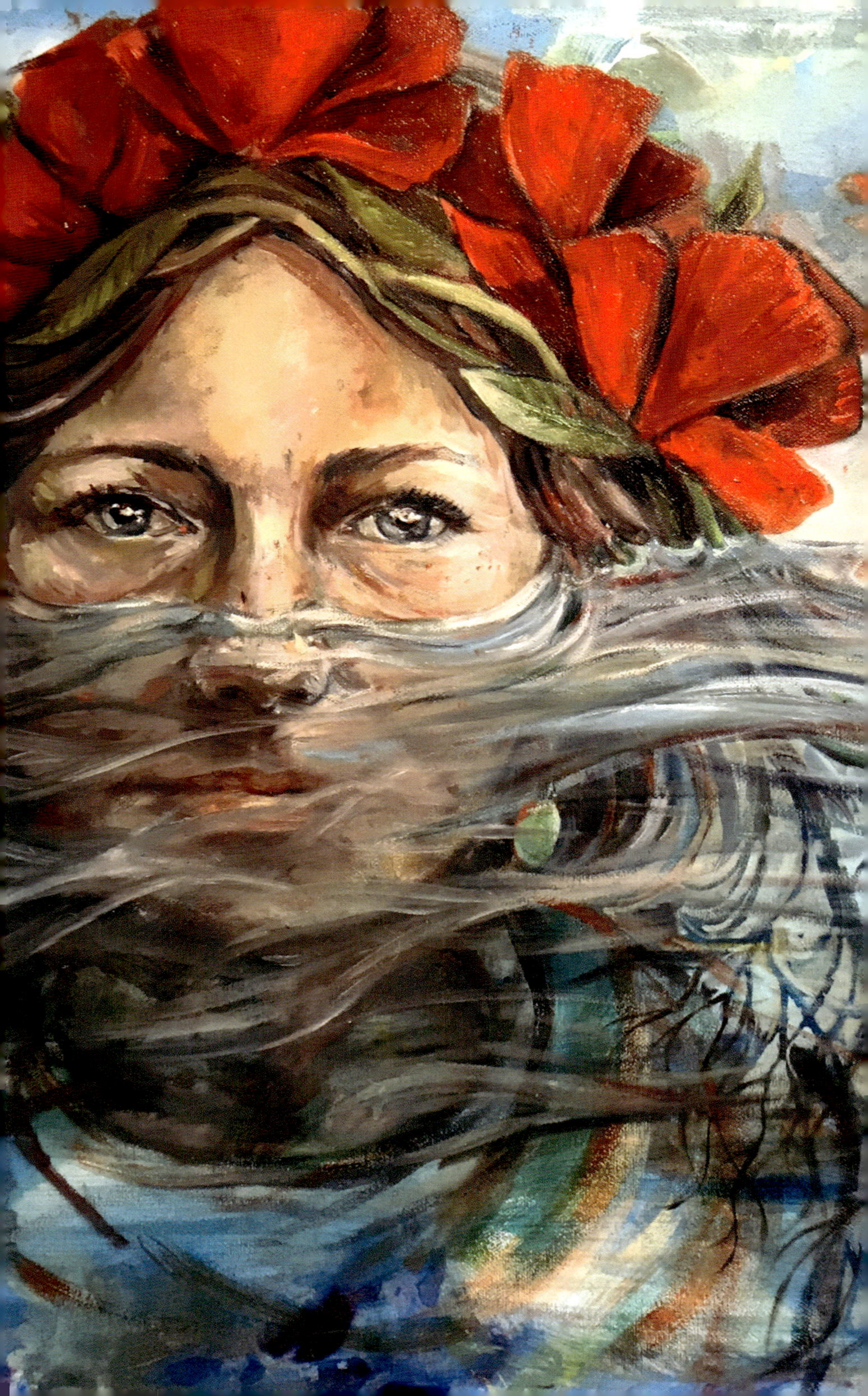

Enoughness

When you start to spiral, feel the sea of unworthiness draw you under, refuse to be swallowed. Do not give your power over to someone else's volatility. You must first belong to yourself, no matter the tides. Destabilized, trust in your ability to discern harmful behaviors. Cast radiant sacred boundary spells for protection. Declare your independence from toxic dynamics. Unclench this futile need to be loved, held, and seen by those unable. Other people's lack of capacity is not a reflection of your worth. Recognize this compulsive grasping, these straws so thin, cannot hold you. Release. You are buoyed by a Source of Love stronger than any swirling current dragging you down. Your enoughness reverberates, an echo carried from the sound of your first breath. Creator's enchanting song. A baptism. Come back to this holy water, immersing yourself, over and over again.

AFFIRMATION

I immerse myself in the holy water of my enoughness
I am buoyed by the Source of Love
Other people's lack of capacity is not a reflection of my worth
I declare my independence from harmful behaviors and toxic dynamics

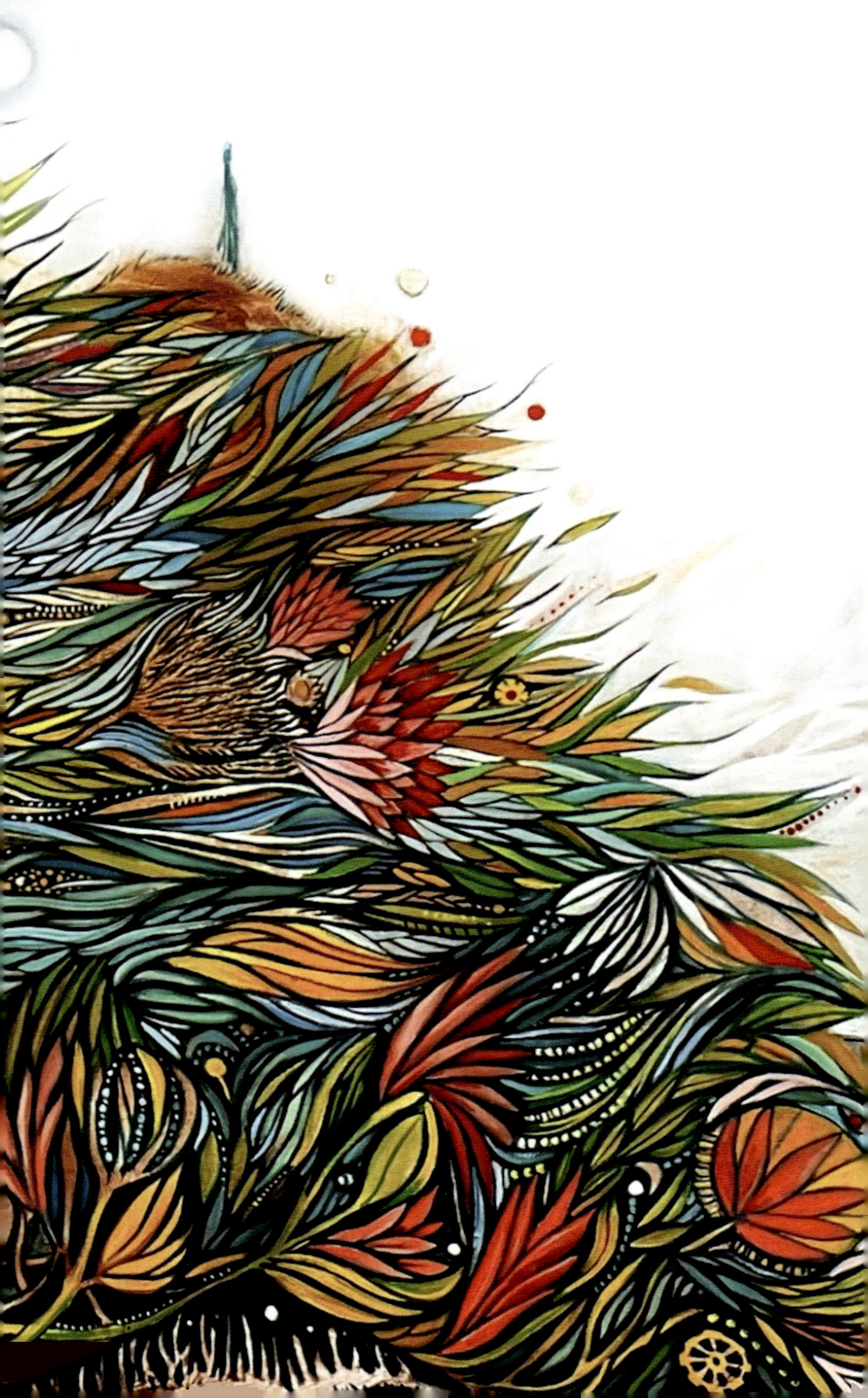

Exhale

What an exquisite thing

An exhalation

AFFIRMATION

I savor the pause found in a tenderhearted exhale
I have space and grace for this sweet release

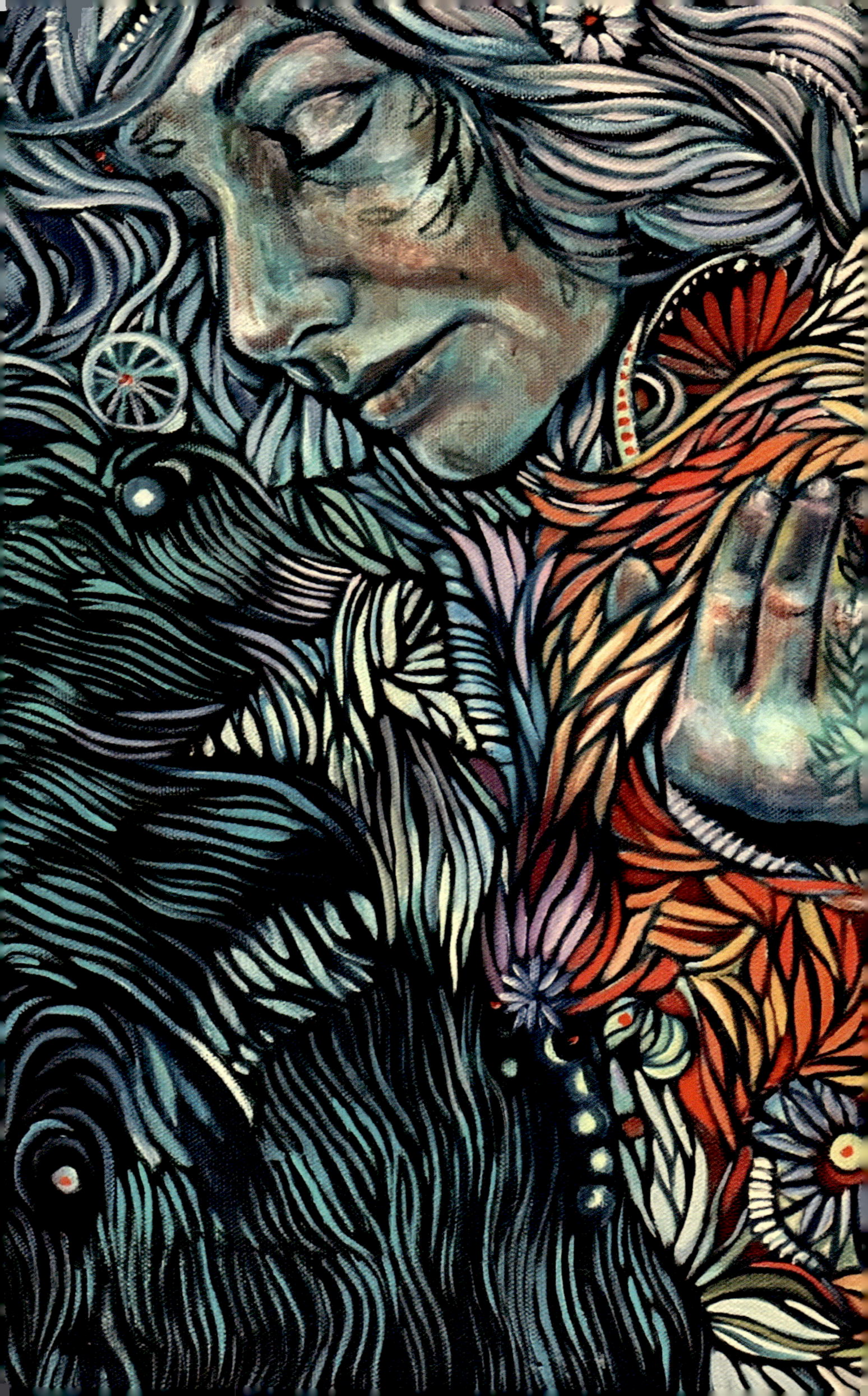

Forgiveness

Not exactly
as you imagined
not a clean slate
no exoneration

A lifting
a ceremony of smoke
from dried cedar leaves
vanishes
morning fog burned off the city fades
revealing every contour of the horizon

From this distance it takes your breath away
you see every ugly gouge clearly
every natural disaster of your life
did not destroy this beauty

And those tender places
that will never be the same
happened out of woundedness
theirs, yours
out of this humanness
that starts in love
and this love
is in us all

AFFIRMATION

I open myself to forgiveness with distance and perspective
I see clearly how human it is to hurt one another from our woundedness
I touch the sacred space in my being undestroyed, beautiful, and whole
regardless of transgressions against me

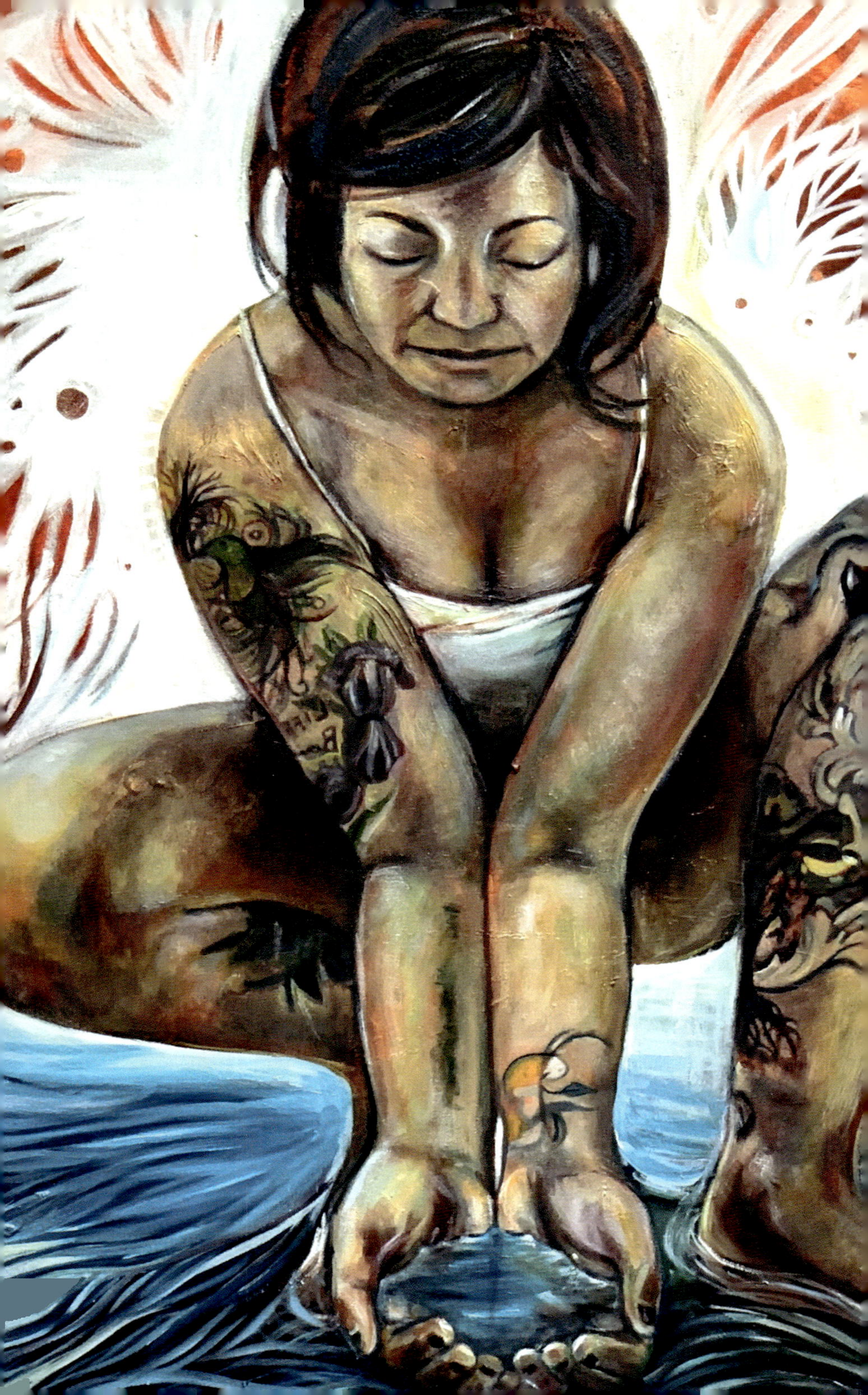

Getting Through

And then you were given this
the last thing you ever wanted to hold

And you find yourself bearing the unbearable weight
somehow

You do not know for how long
you feel your body shaking under the heaviness
vibrating with the horror

But even more, you feel the pulse, the sinew of everything else
you have endured, the strength of all that you are made of, this
is wrapped around your being, carries you forward

You remember there is always an end, the other side
you are being shaped through this, awakened to yourself
you gather all the lessons, the goodness you can scrape off
of this moment

And you know exactly what you need to do
to get through

AFFIRMATION

I know what to do to get through

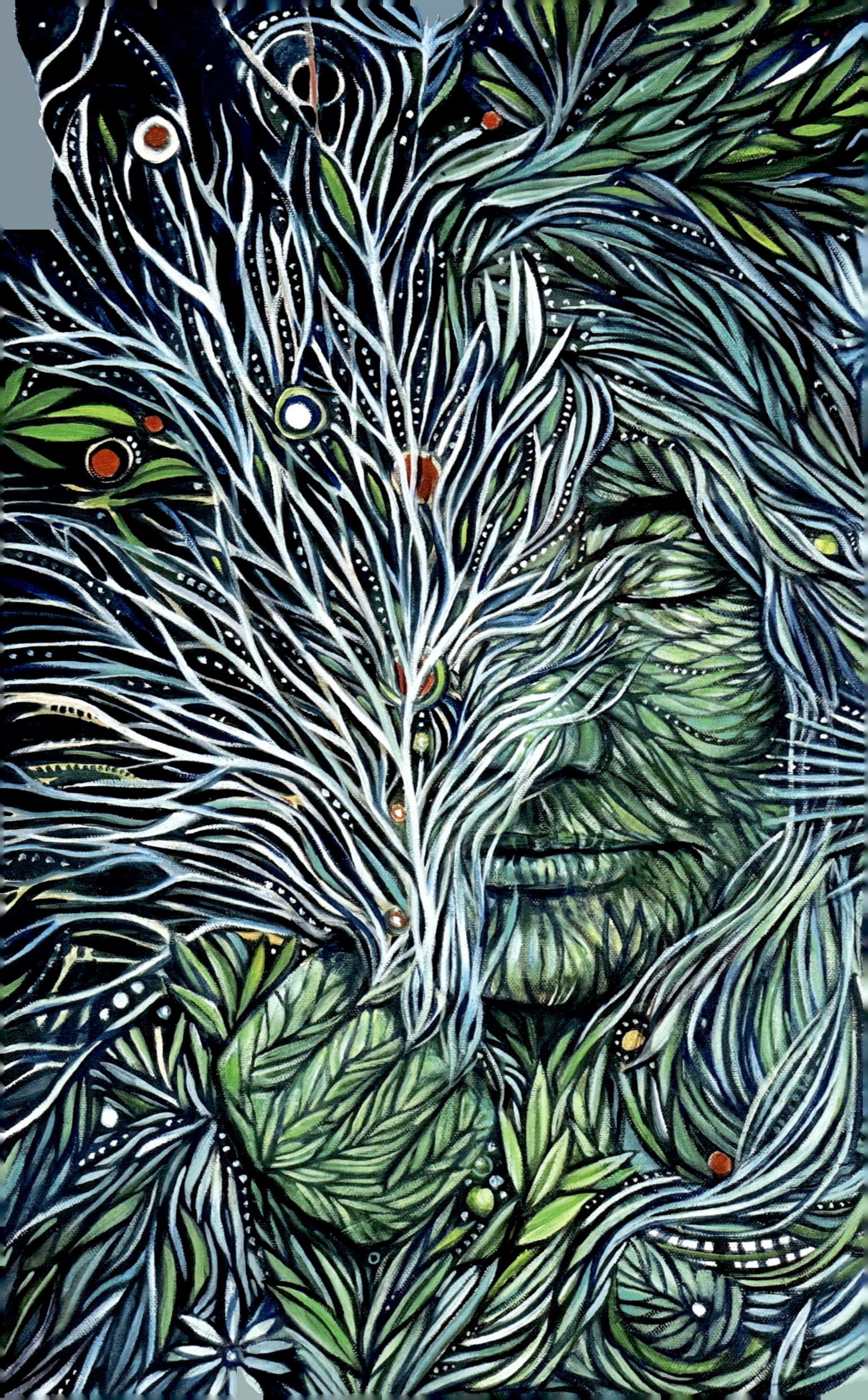

Gratitude

As you retrace your life, notice blessings
blossoming suddenly in your being
until there is a full tree in bloom in your heart
white dogwood flowers with wide open mouths
singing to you about joy

And there are also experiences of difficulty
of pain and terrible loss
these too are not for nothing

Bright red apples fallen, bruised and rotting
give themselves completely to the earth and the worms

Let go of what was or could have been
hold what is
sow these seeds, an offering of nourishment
for the next season

Offer gratitude also for darker moments
they too are a powerful part
of your becoming

AFFIRMATION

I retrace the blessings of my life
appreciate their blossoming
I feel the swell of gratitude open
joy in full bloom in my heart

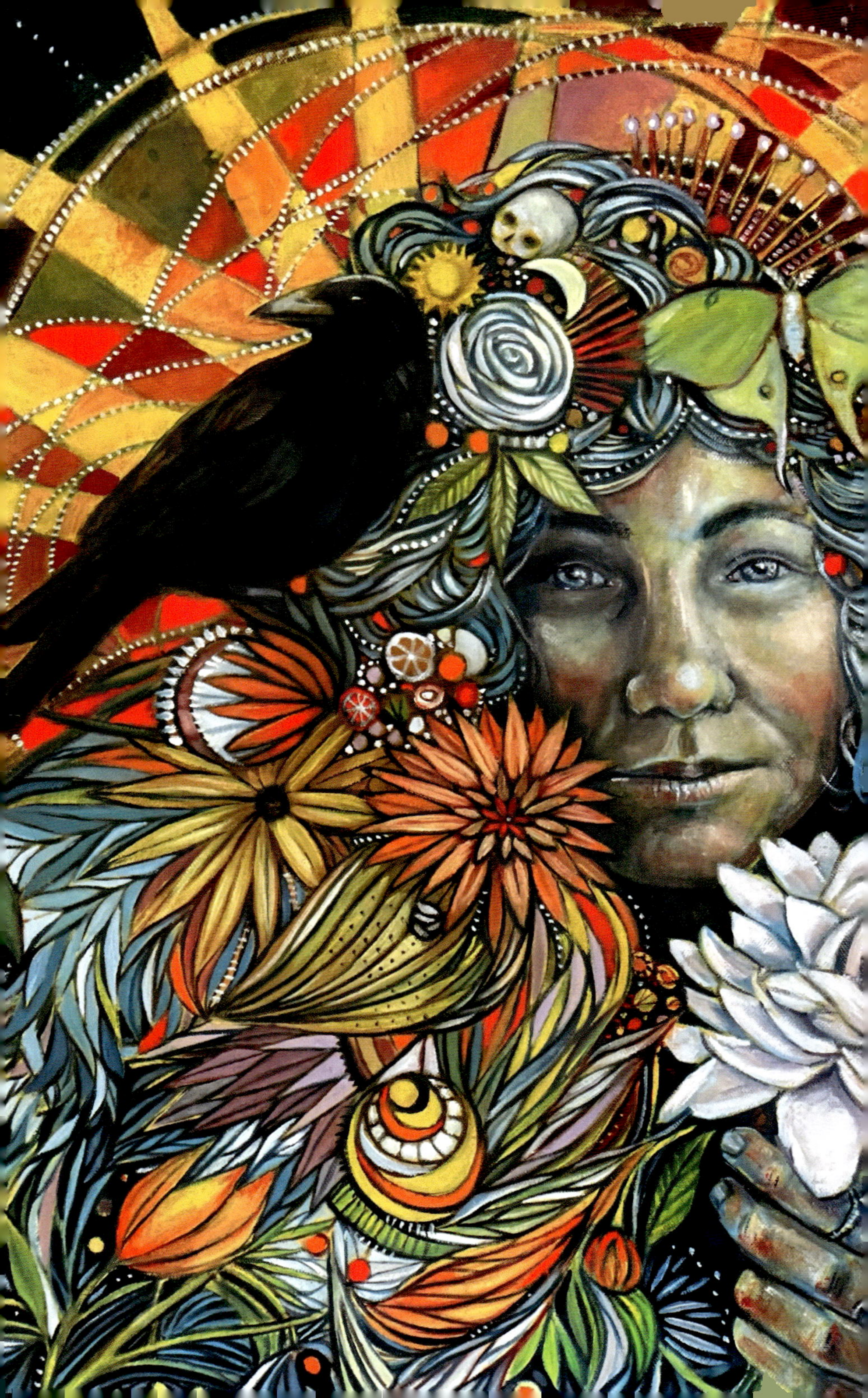

Harvest Moon Wisdom

As we transition to more darkness, the harvest moon
illuminates, urges you to pause
to reflect on where you are at in your life.

What has come to fruition?

Where have you arrived, actualized, realized?

What metaphorical crops are ready
to be harvested in your life? In your being?

What is right here, now
for you to enjoy, savor, devour?

What can you gather, appreciate, and bottle up or can
for a future, darker, and colder season?

Are there longings, truths, insights, awarenesses
that could go to waste in the dark
in the shadows of yourself?

How can you take the time and attention
to notice, integrate, and harvest
for your nourishment, growth, and awakening?

What if all you have been through can be tended to and used
for a vibrant, colorful feast at the table of your holy life?

AFFIRMATION

I pause to bear witness to the growth I have realized
I joyfully savor the abundant harvest
set at the holy table of my life

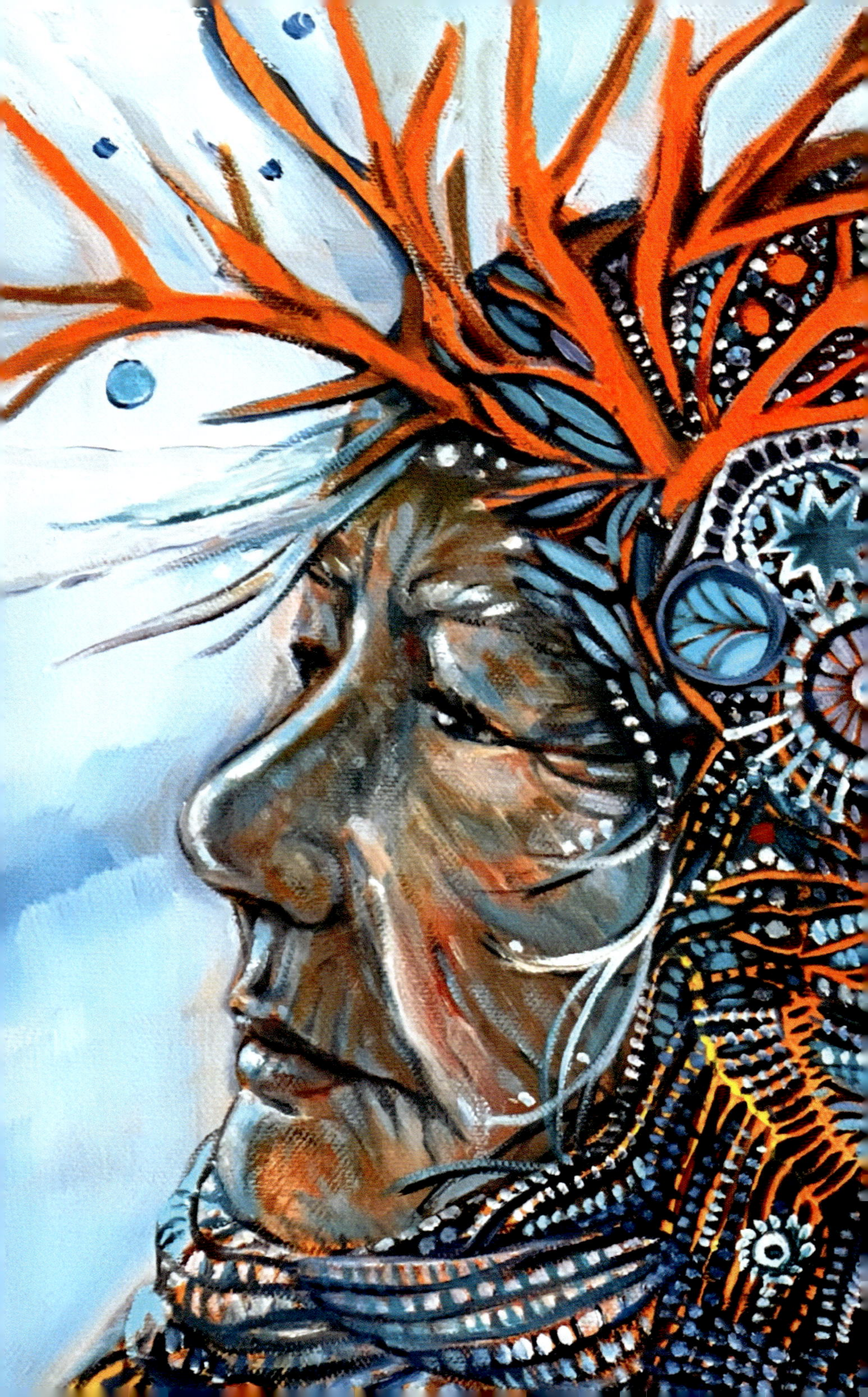

Healing

Although it is spring
and the snow has melted
this single dignified icicle holds
onto the great white oak
with all its might
gleaming and sharp as a wolf's tooth
hanging in the shadows of tree branches
carries the magic of winter
wonders of glinting raw
sharp unapologetic grief

A steady drip from the thaw
the melting
the letting go
a slow tender weeping

Love doesn't die
it transforms
ice becomes water
evaporates to vapor
drawn up to the sky
an offering
a prayer
of floating white clouds
in a sea of blue above
the eventual rain
a generous
heaving release
from the great mystery
that holds us all

AFFIRMATION

I trust the unique timing of my healing

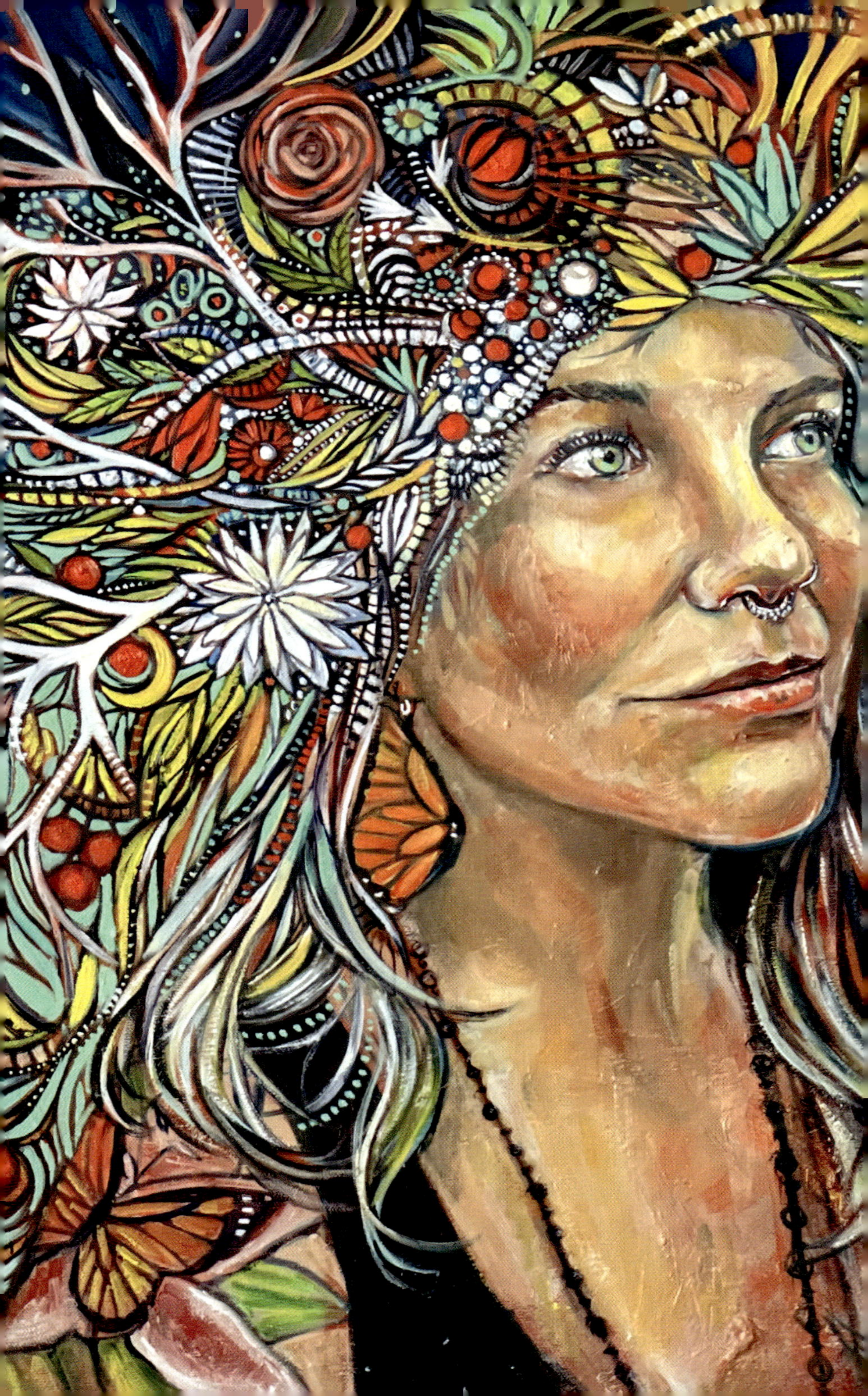

Heart of Creation

I fiercely commit to be wholly present to
what is happening in my life, my community, and this world.

I will not turn my face away from even the most horrific.
I trust my eyes to adjust to its brightness so that I may see clearly.

I want to always, always shed the number of tears
proportionate to what is before me.

I honor that there is an infinite well from which I draw
that taps into the Heart of Creation
connected through my own beating heart
unfurling endless compassion, care, and courage.

I am fueled and ready to do whatever I can
from my place on this planet.

I know there is no act of kindness too small to offer.
With each breath I will continue to offer, and offer, and offer.
I will sow love with even the tiniest seeds I hold.

AFFIRMATION

My heart is connected to the Heart of Creation
I sow love with even the tiniest seeds I hold

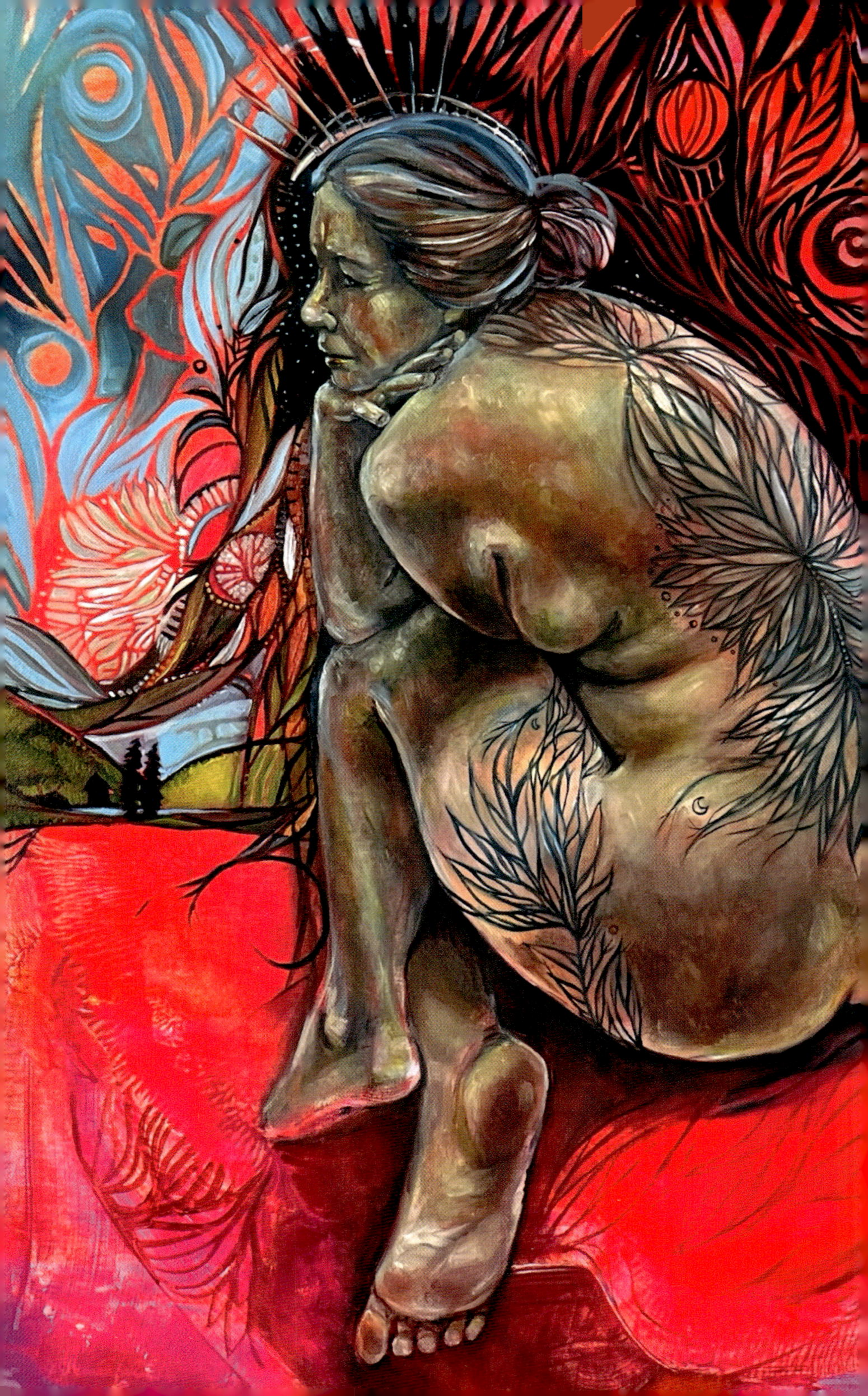

Home of Belonging

There are some things that may help you remember.
Sacred rituals. Loved ones circling around you.
Holding you up. Reflecting love. Lighting candles in
your holy name. On knees, bowing with hands at heart.
Whispering prayers. Singing and rejoicing in praise.
Dancing in circles together.

You are already held in this endless web, you have simply
forgotten. This home of belonging is a remembering,
a returning to settle in magnificent infinite arms
that hold you regardless. Tender whispers of truth
reverberate in your bones,"You are enough, dear one!"

Notice how the sun rises every single day
indiscriminately pouring light on all of us, giving life
even in darkness. The moon catches her luminous glow
throwing this brilliant love back to us.

The trees, flowers, and plants
even ragged, twisted, and broken
receive this light without question
rest in the earth
cradled in knowing
they are Beloved.

Why then cannot you?

AFFIRMATION

I am cradled in the arms of the Beloved
I am always held in this home of belonging

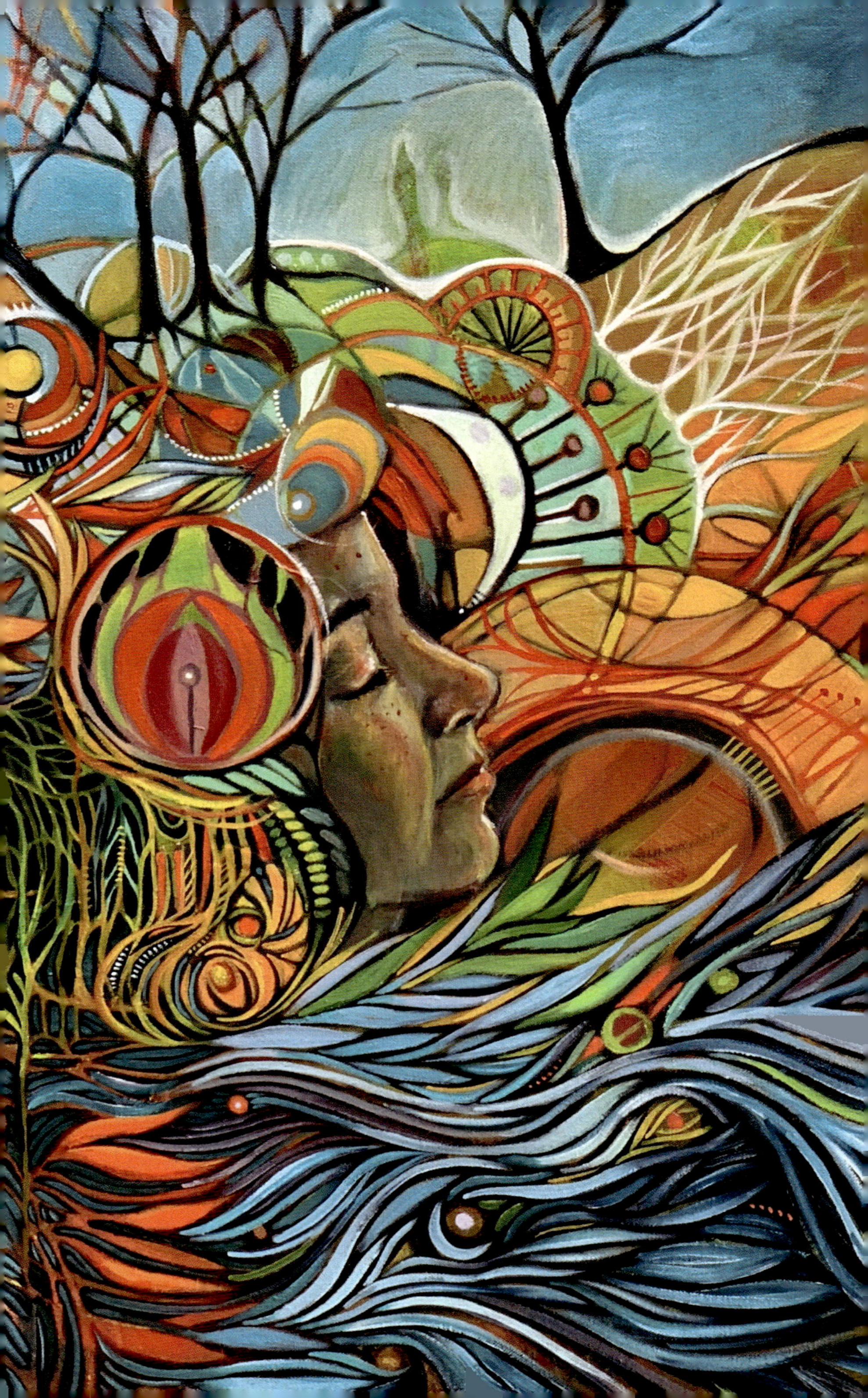

Homecoming

When you begin to name your traumas
they start singing in deep lush enchanted forests
you never knew existed in you
and you travel great lengths
holding a lantern out in front of you
on a dark path
only a small patch of bouncing light
in many middle of the night journeys
just to follow their beautiful voices

How they have so many songs
so much to tell you, and it somehow
makes your foot begin to tap unexpected
makes your body move
in strange ways, all hips and sway
shaking like some sort of exorcism
gyrating and beginning to sing along
holding your hands up
in a peculiar type of worship
that can only have been handed down
through your ancestors

And although it seems so far away
somehow you are more home now
than you have ever been

AFFIRMATION

I lovingly name my traumas
I listen to their wise-wound songs
I move with their particular music
that calls me home to myself

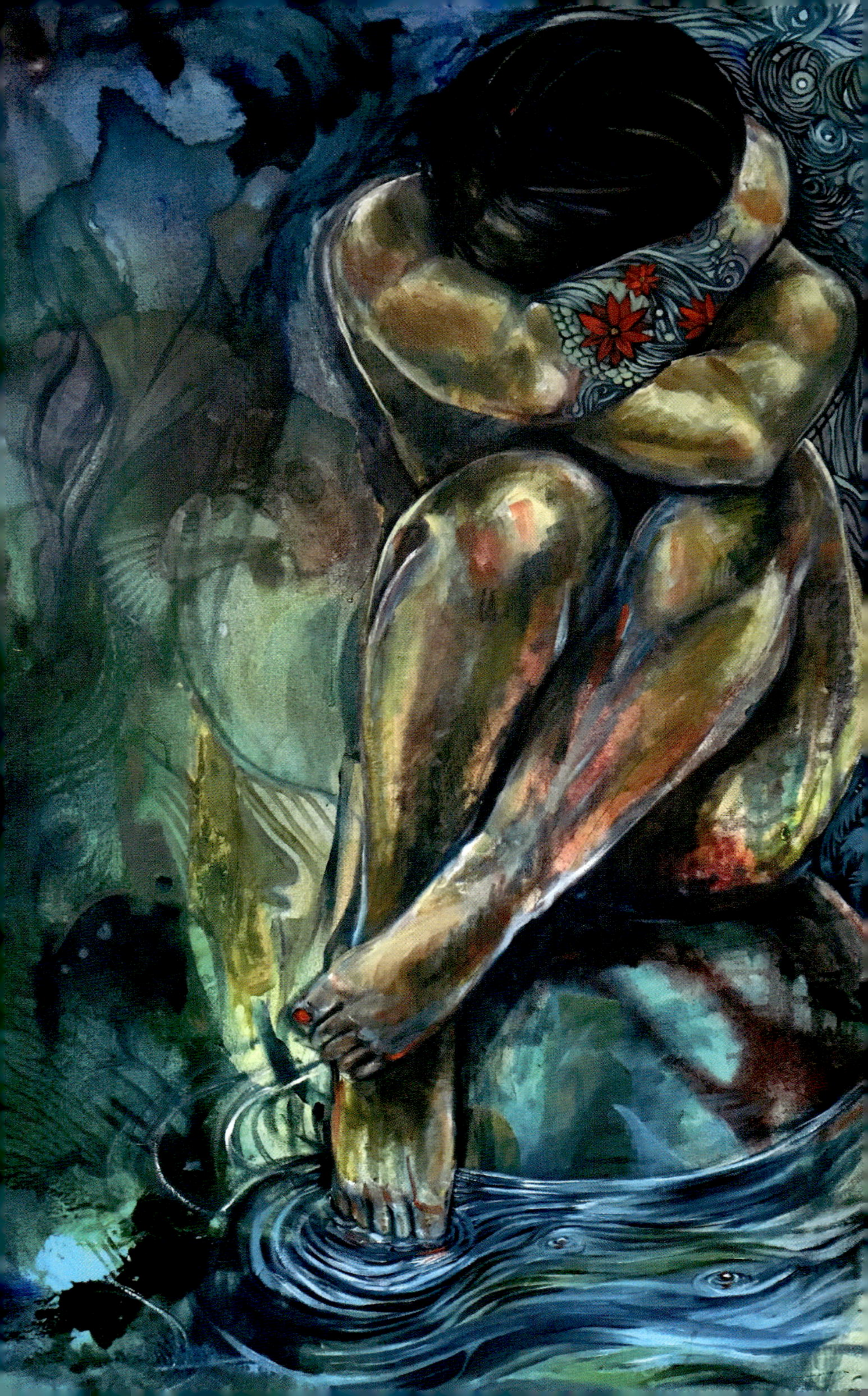

How Human of Me

I meet my humanness with fierce compassion
utter again and again, my own tender hand on my heart
"how human of me"
as many times as is needed

From this gentle place of clarity and love
I begin again and again

AFFIRMATION

How human of me
I did my best, I release the rest
I vow to begin again

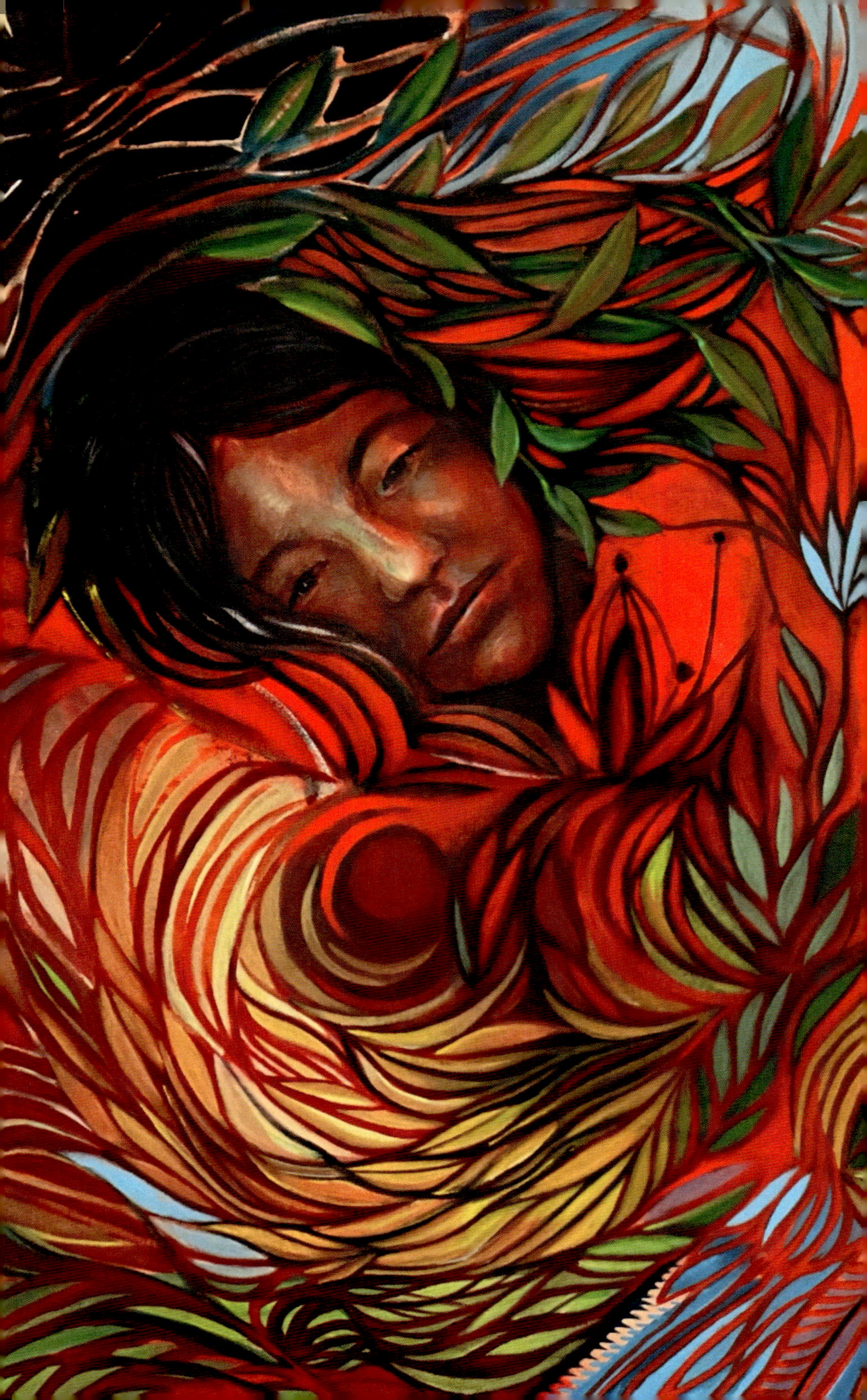

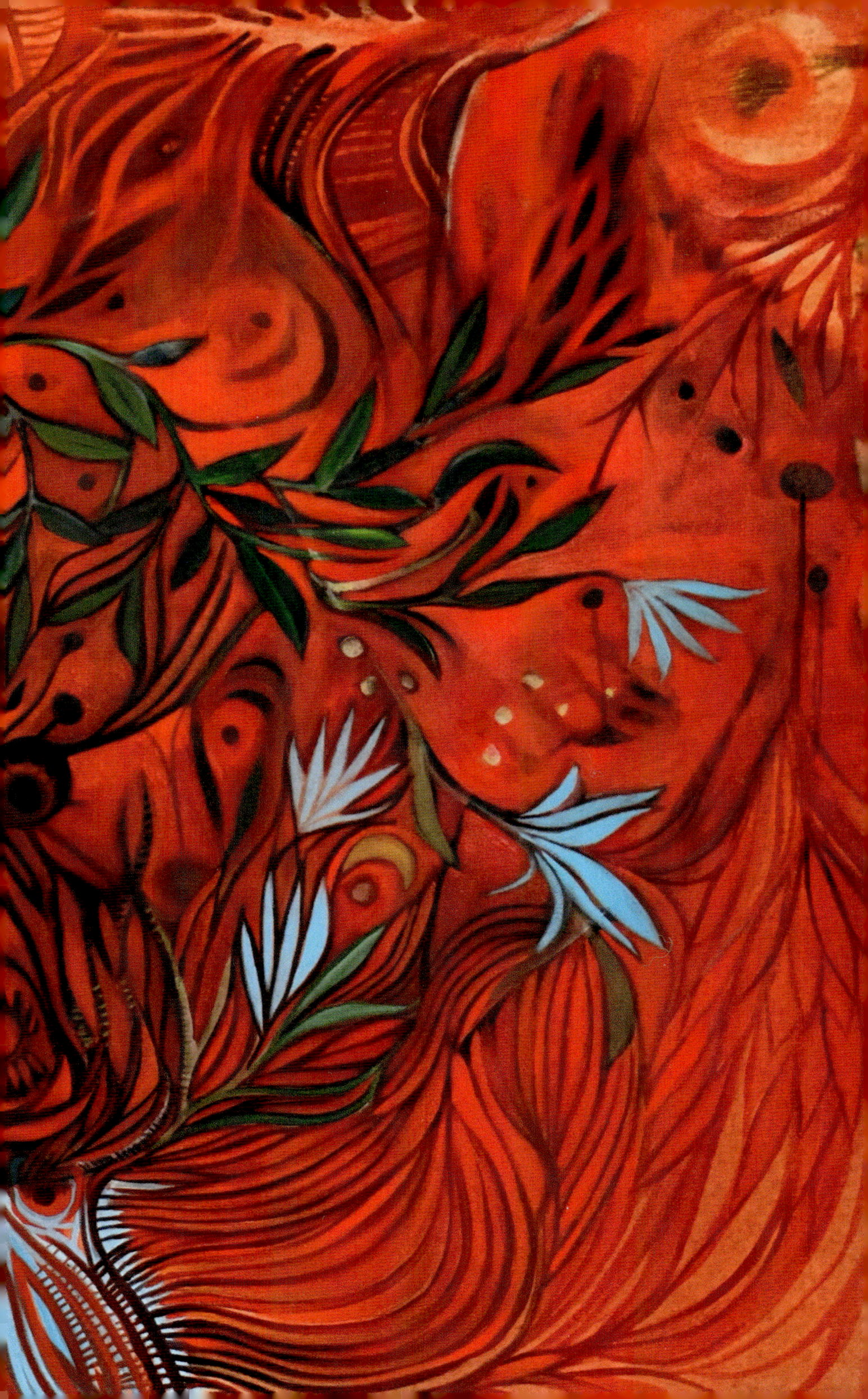

How to be Free

When your body has been clenched
for as long as you can remember
but you didn't even realize

A reflex to your trauma
to all the ways people have hurt you

Protection, tension knotted
knitted up like a chain link fence
this tortoise shell with knobby ridges
you live inside

The world has not always been safe
your body remembers, knows
it had to be a balled up fist
ready to fight, to punch, to keep you alive

It makes sense doesn't it?
This brave way your body
has carried these truths
has helped you survive everything
to this moment

Whisper
(hand on your heart)
"Thank you my body, my star, my gem
you have saved my life more times than I can count
and I am still here, still here
living
because of you"
I want to reteach you
(as long as it takes, as many times as you forget)
how to be free
how to unlock this fear
you have held so conscientiously
to show you, you are no longer there
you are safe now
you are here
breathe easy my love
soften
right now
no one is here to hurt you

AFFIRMATION

I am safe, I am free
I can soften and breathe easy

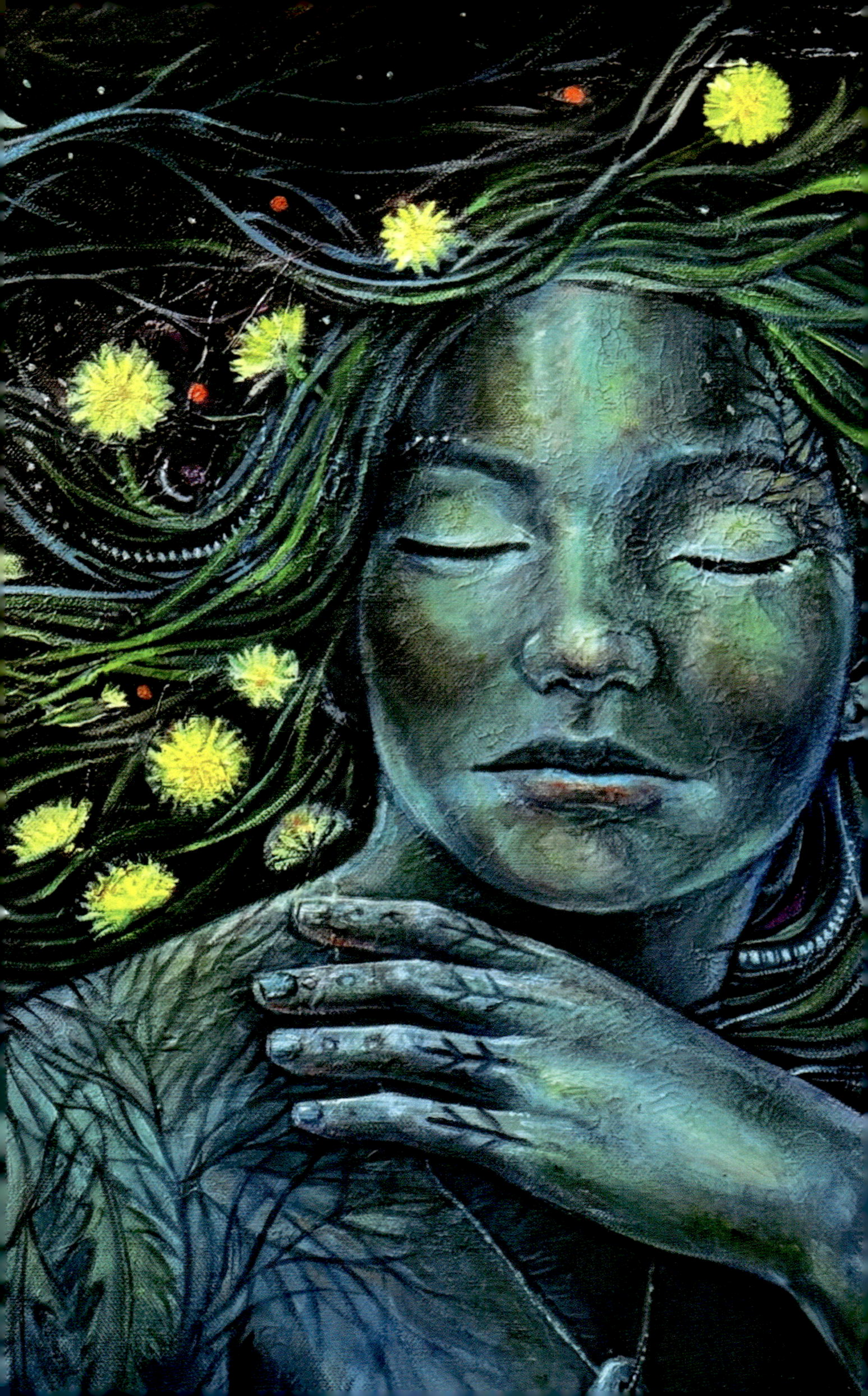

I Am the Dandelion

I am the dandelion
all yellow petals falling away
unveiling soft white wispy
flower full of seeds

I hold close for this moment
a part of me I know
I must let go
allow to float away
on the winds of this world
land wherever it is you may
bless you to become whoever you will
and love you for always

AFFIRMATION

I lovingly shepherd you along your own path
blessing you to become who you will on your own terms
I release control and support the flow of your unfolding journey

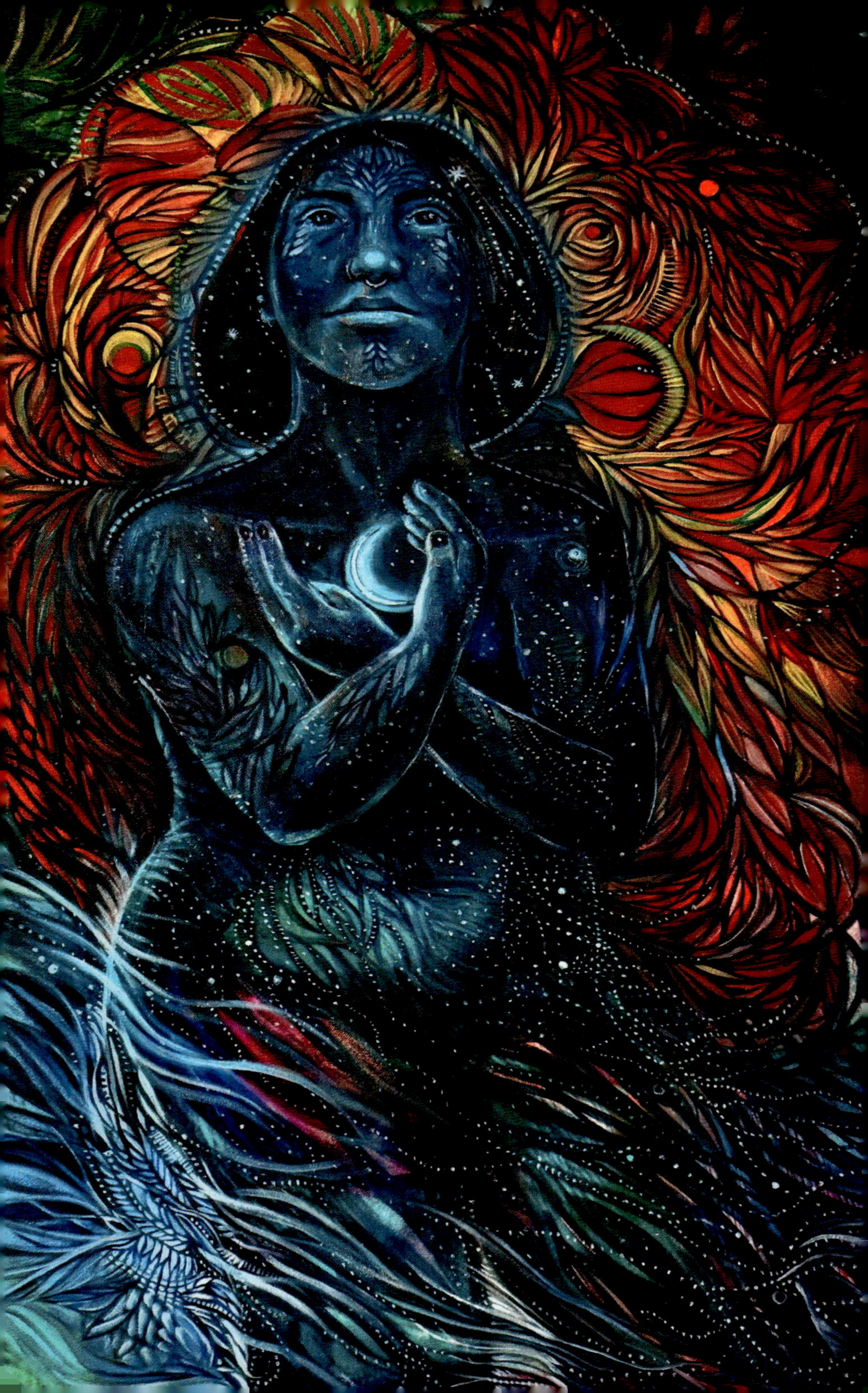

Irrevocable Wholeness

And just like you
the moon has always
been whole

No matter how much
sunlight is striking its skin

Even if just a crescent
of shimmering light
you do not have to be
full to shine

Every inch of you
already exists, even if
held in sacred darkness
waiting to be revealed

AFFIRMATION

I reclaim my birthright and connect to my
shimmering Irrevocable Wholeness
I trust in darkness as a sacred space of gestation
for the cultivation of my gifts and revelation
of my soul's unique purpose

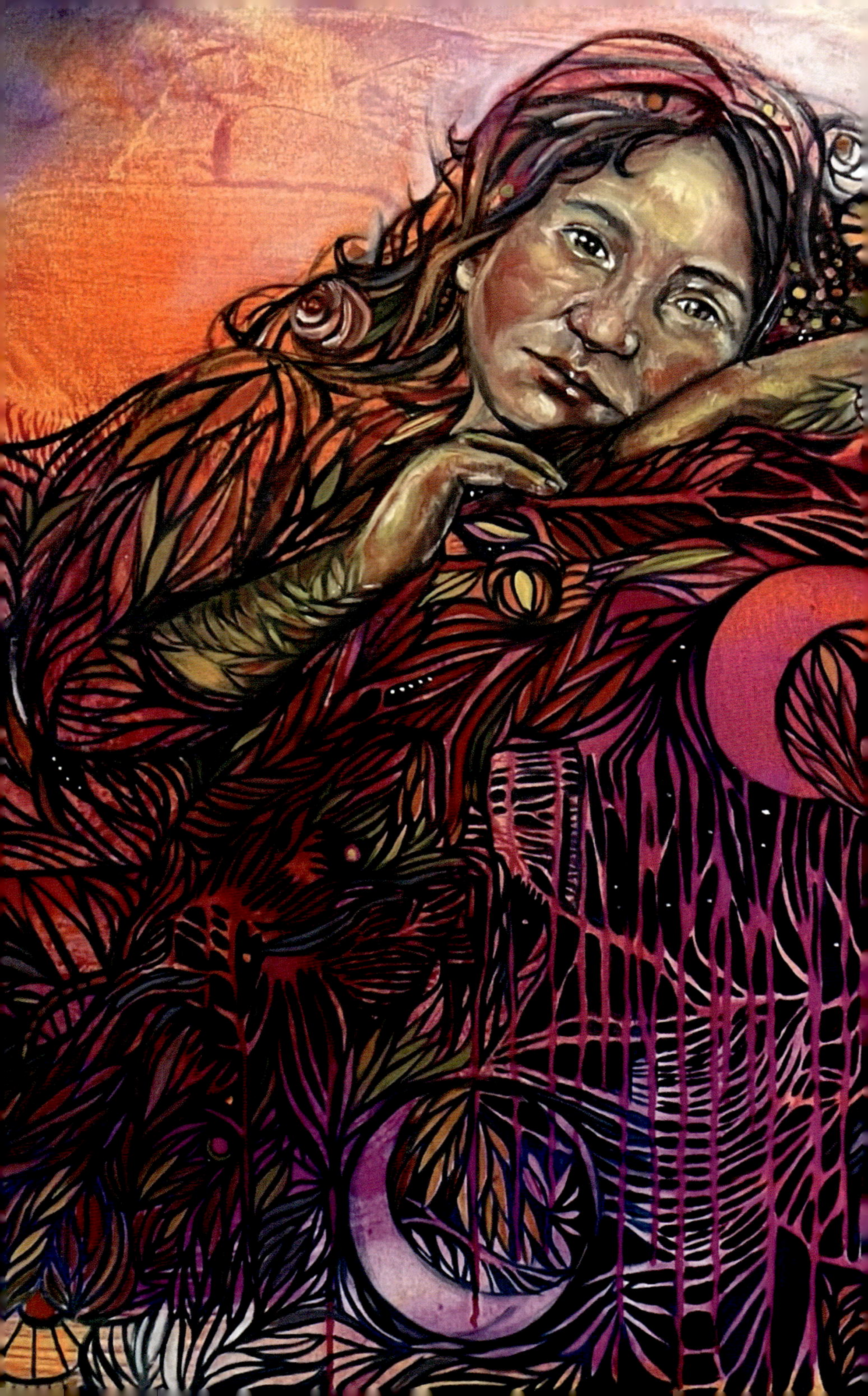

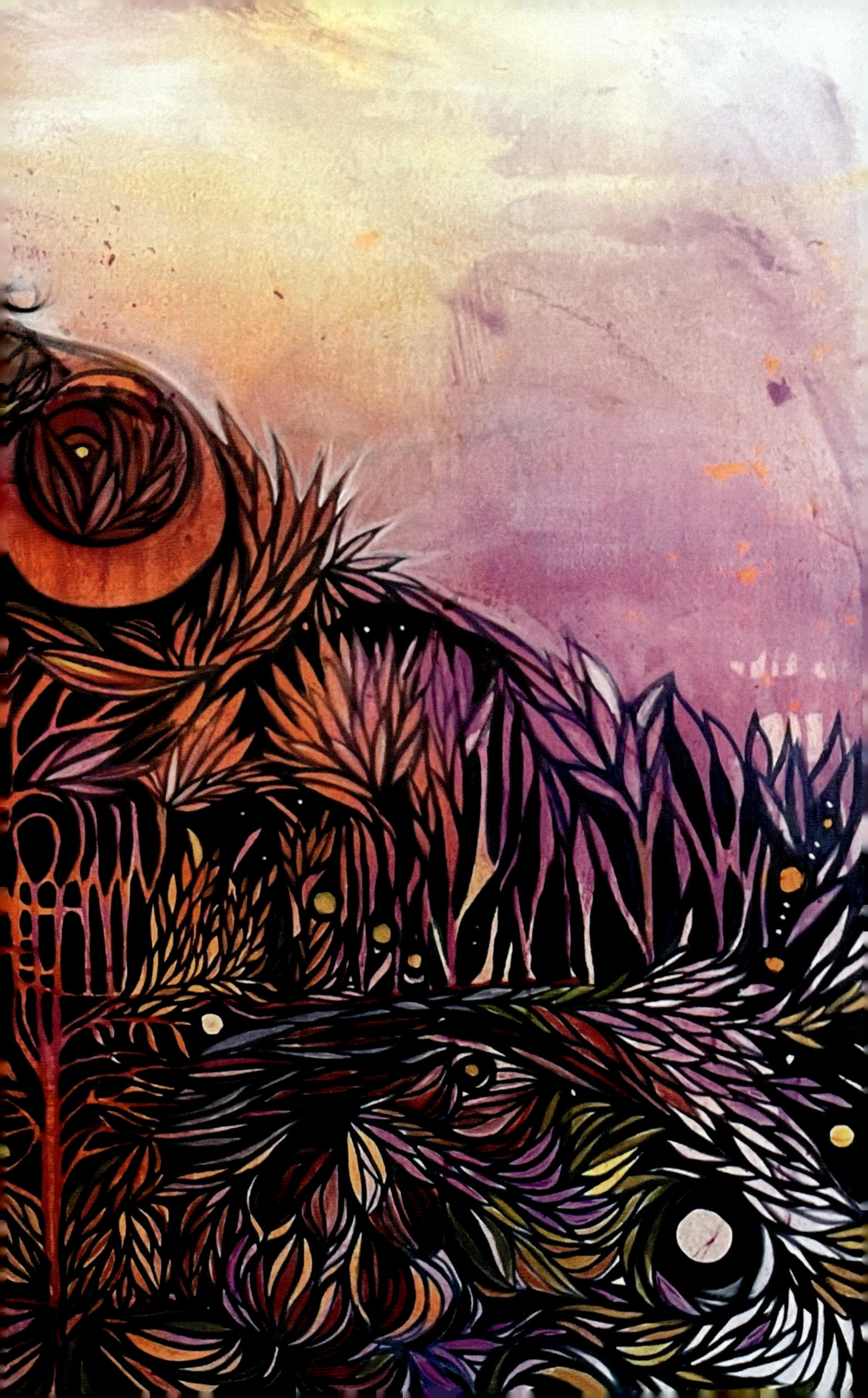

Lacuna

Healing is the steady
shifting of seasons
the great wheel of life turning
and churning
forward
indiscriminate of
the ugly, the beautiful
the in-between
taking it all in

The body of the earth
with her thick dark soil
honors all that is given

What if we too see
life's offerings like this
cracked egg shell
peach pit
flower petals
rotten strawberries
rancid moldy apple
sharp to the touch
stinging our eyes
received as nourishment
understanding the time
and effort
it takes to decompose
soften, crumble
become one with us
transforming to
miraculous fertile ground
to sweet possibility

AFFIRMATION

I honor the profound offerings of my life
no matter how sharp, painful, and unbearable,
I receive what has been given
to transform me in beautiful and unexpected ways

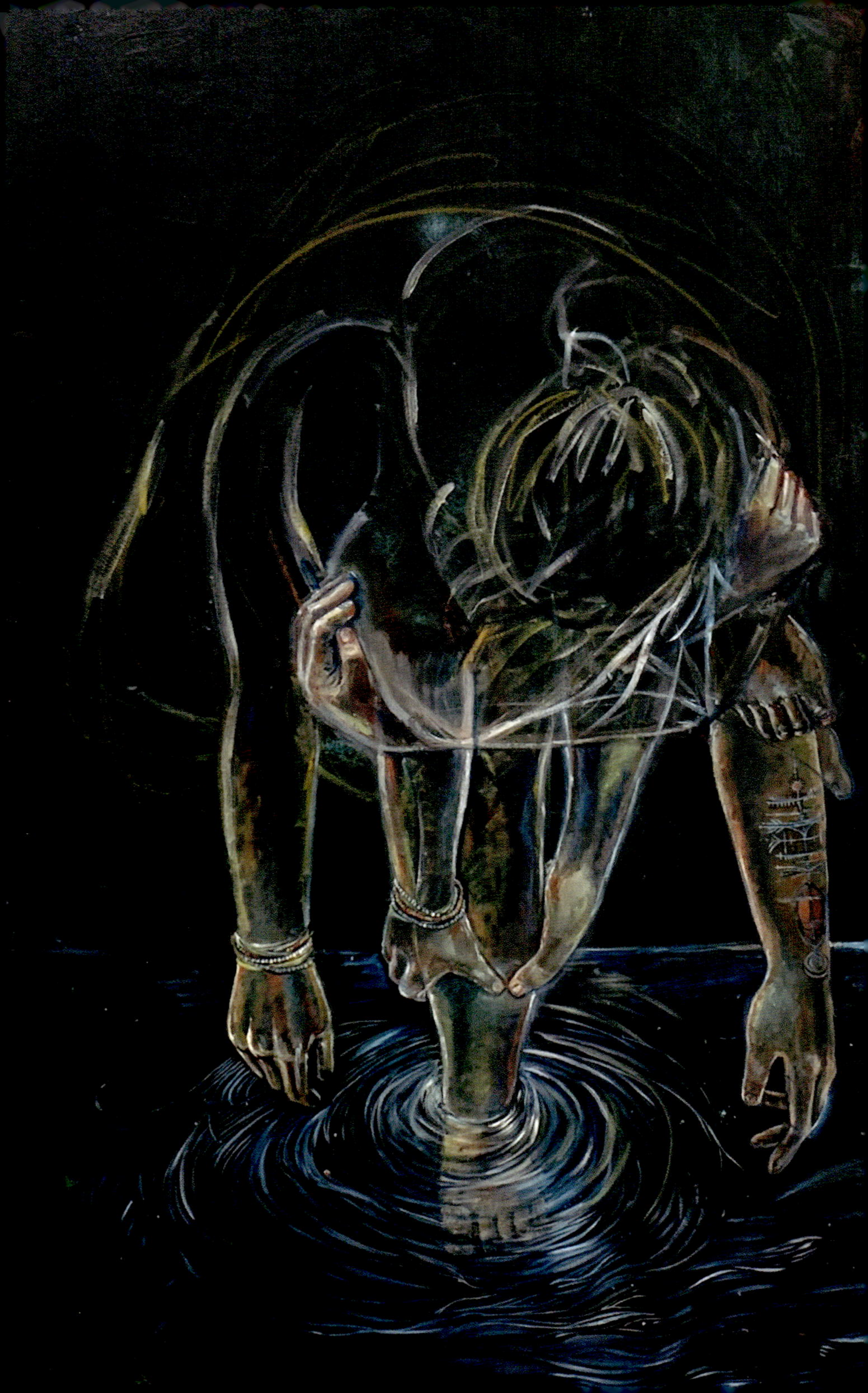

Lamentation

This grief is a different flavor of pain
laced with the rage it took to know
the ending was inevitable
the anger, a fire needed to burn the ties

It takes cool water to calm the flames
bowing at the firesite to bear witness
you watch the dark ashes carried away by wind

It requires laying down sword and armor to bury
in a gravesite you dig
with your own hands
cry as much as you need
visit as often as you must
this headstone exists in you
difficult things happened here
bring flowers to honor the love and the loss
repeat a prayer on forgiving our trespasses
as many times as is needed
bless the fact that some things may never make sense
and this is part of living
brush off the dirt
listen intently
appreciate the wisdom in
the midnight blue-black Raven's
mournful caws
these striking calls
an ending

AFFIRMATION

I lament endings
and take the necessary time and actions
to honor the love and the loss
I bless the stark truth of this painful severing and
unhook from the hurt to forgive our trespasses

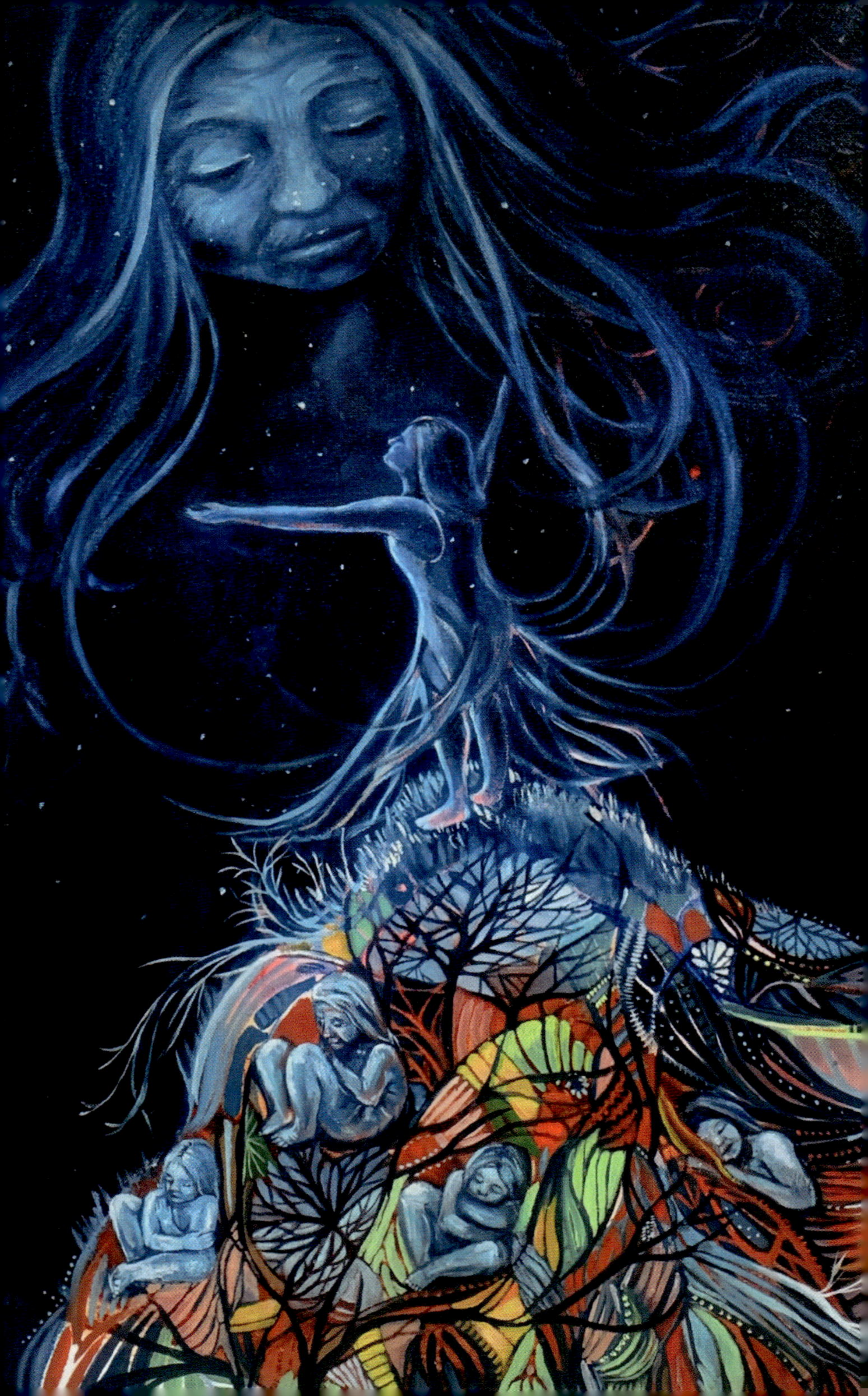

Lifted Up

Once

Broken

I visited a healer, she prayed over me
said, "there is a crowd of Angels surrounding you
they've been clapping since the time of your birth"

It took me years to hear their hands
lifting me up with their music

AFFIRMATION

I am held, loved, supported, and lifted up

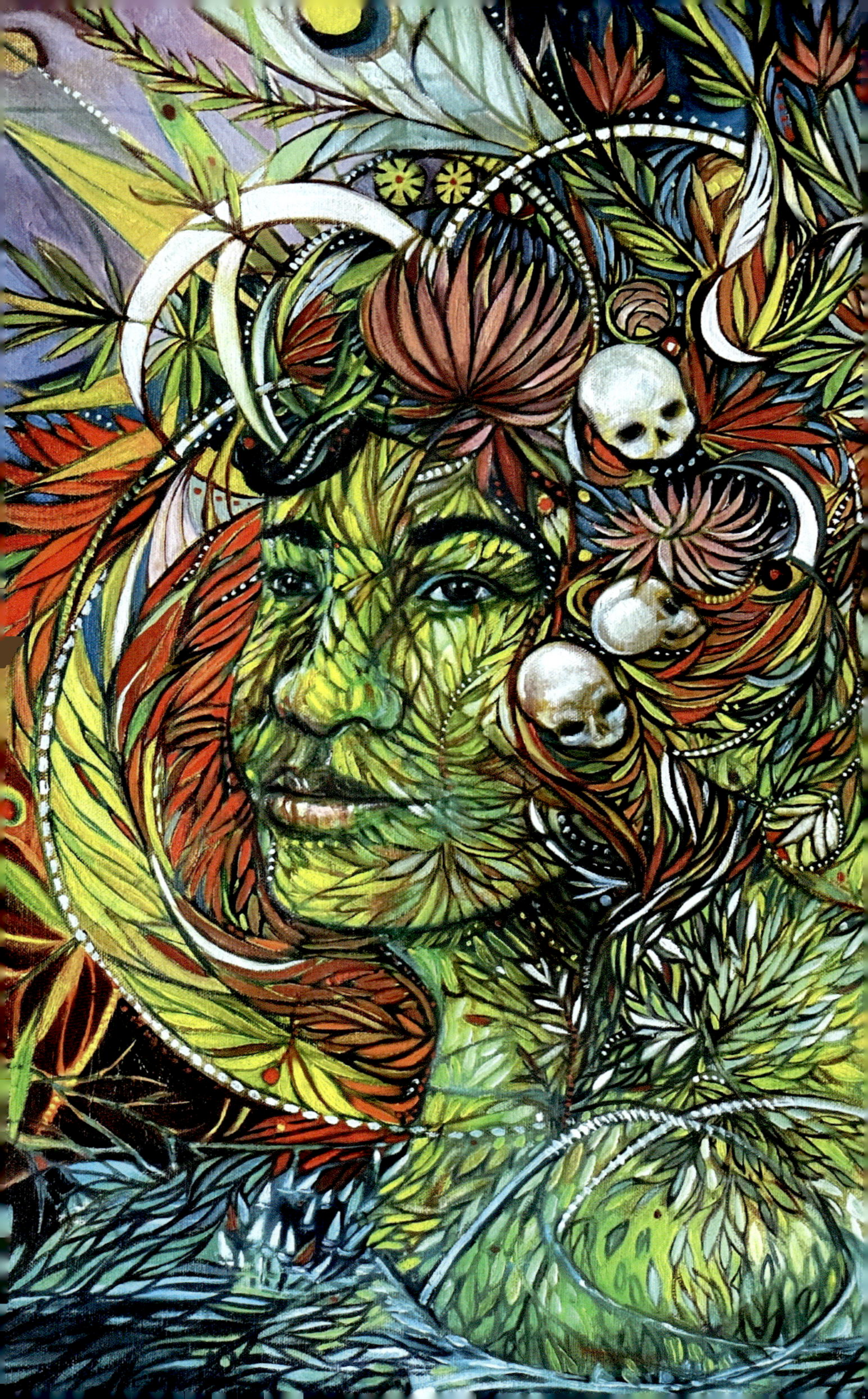

Map of the World

If your life is a body of water
contained in its own unique
crevice of the world
and you were formed from
the Source of all water
just like all of us, all of us

Connected but individual
and although you have
your own separate name
each of us, each of us
if we unroll the Map of the World
we can see, we see clearly
one creek flows into the
next river into
the next ocean
and it is endless and circular

No matter how large or small
or long or short our existence
we are here, we are alive
here, now

What kindness will you drop
into this place?
What tenderness will ripple out
from you during your brief time on earth?
What glimmers of love will gleam
across the surface of your being?
What wondrous waves of beauty
will you form and unfurl?

AFFIRMATION

I recognize and honor our interconnectedness
I realize the power of my presence
I leave kindness, tenderness, love, and beauty in my wake

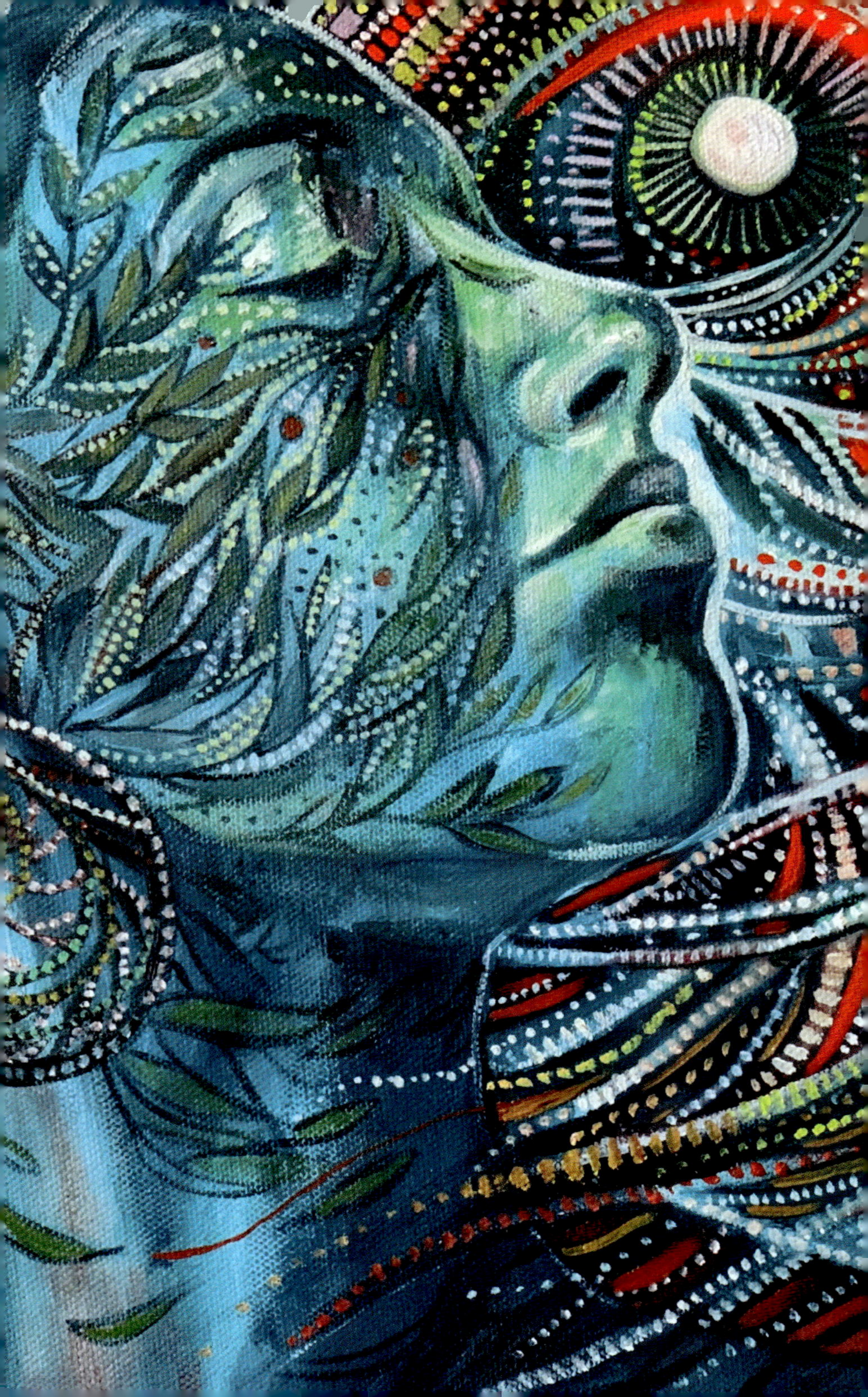

Mirror

This is a form of love, a mirror
like a dark lake that grabs the moon by
gorgeous iridescent cheeks
looks directly into your eyes
declares
"You are a bright light!"

And something deep within you heals
as you traverse the underworld
visit this ancient ruin for the last time
leave flowers and scribbled love letters
at the gravesites of all the parts of you
that believed themselves unworthy

Return somehow reborn
shining

AFFIRMATION

I choose people who see me wholly
and mirror back to me my worth
I am a bright beautiful light
I reciprocate and reflect this love

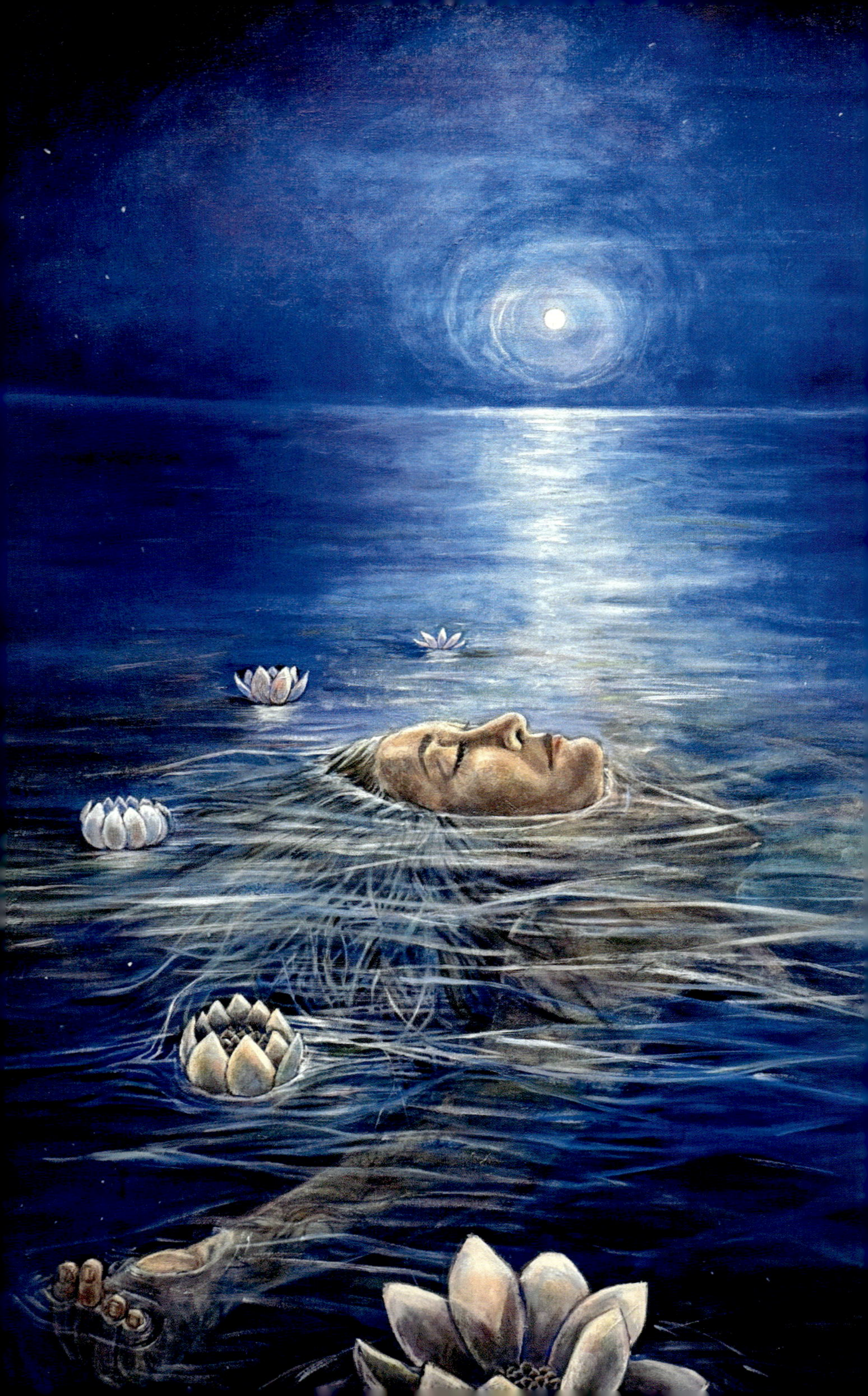

Ocean of Knowing

May I travel to the place beyond thoughts
drink from the Ocean of Knowing
where it is a wordless nothing
and all the words spoken
of everything all at once

May I commune with
Truth

AFFIRMATION

I am connected to the Ocean of Knowing

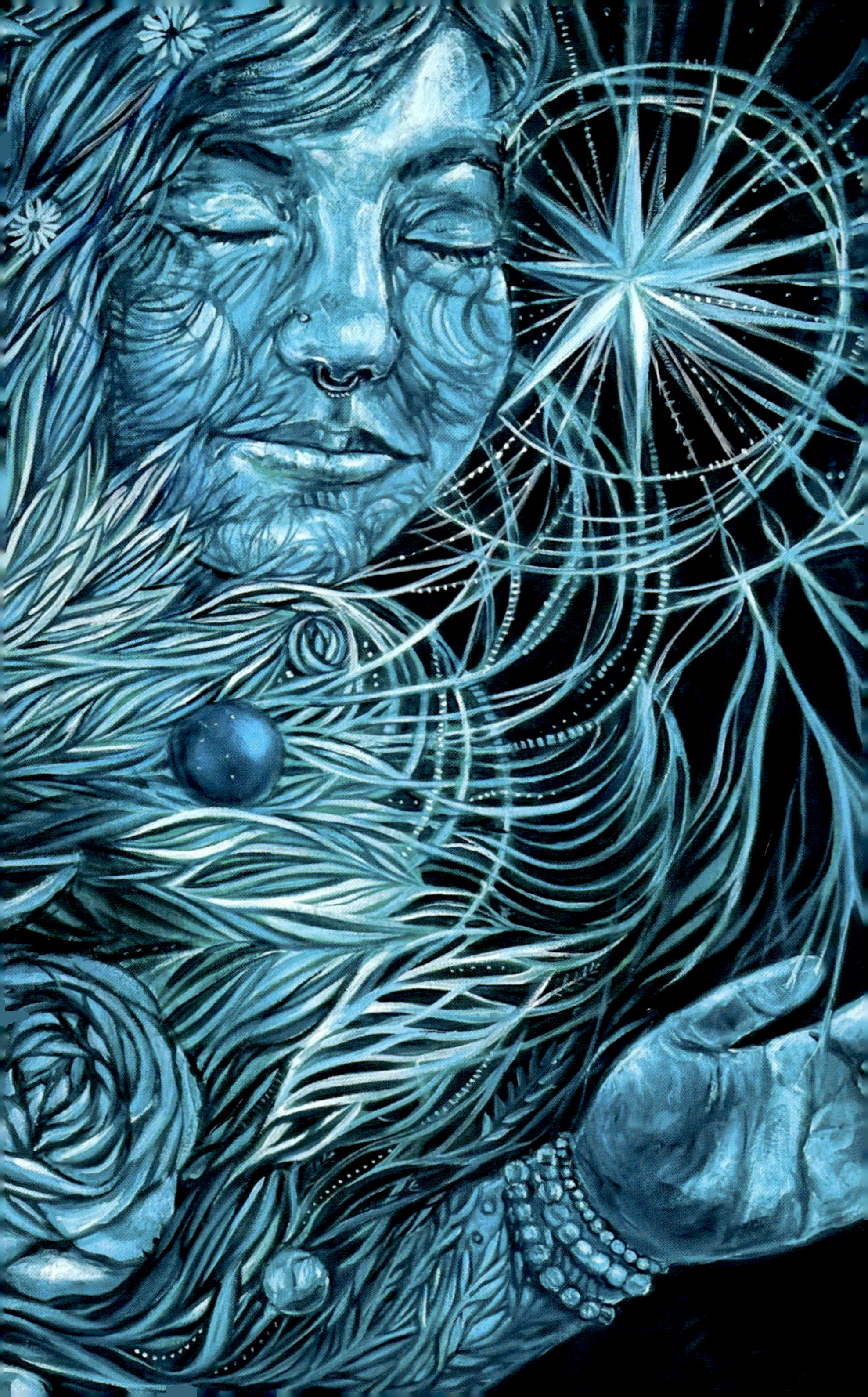

Ocean Songs

After years below
looking up at the water's dark surface
sensing cycles of life above
the faraway touch of sunlight
distant waxing and waning
moonlight
her longing
a gravitational pull
tides of something more
beyond her grasp

An eventual refusal to remain
she moves upwards
looking back at
the severed rope that tied her
to a life she would no longer endure
frayed strands unbraiding, surrendering
their power to the undulations
and swirling currents of the past

It has been a slow departure
from all that held her down
she feels herself rise up, float as if weightless
break the surface
gulp the air
walk into the knowing arms of the world
finally arriving at loving herself
singing songs of the ocean

AFFIRMATION

I recognize the things, spaces, and people that hold me back and down
I have the courage necessary to break patterns and break free
I have the discernment to know when to alter choices, relationships, or cut ties
I trust my inner-compass

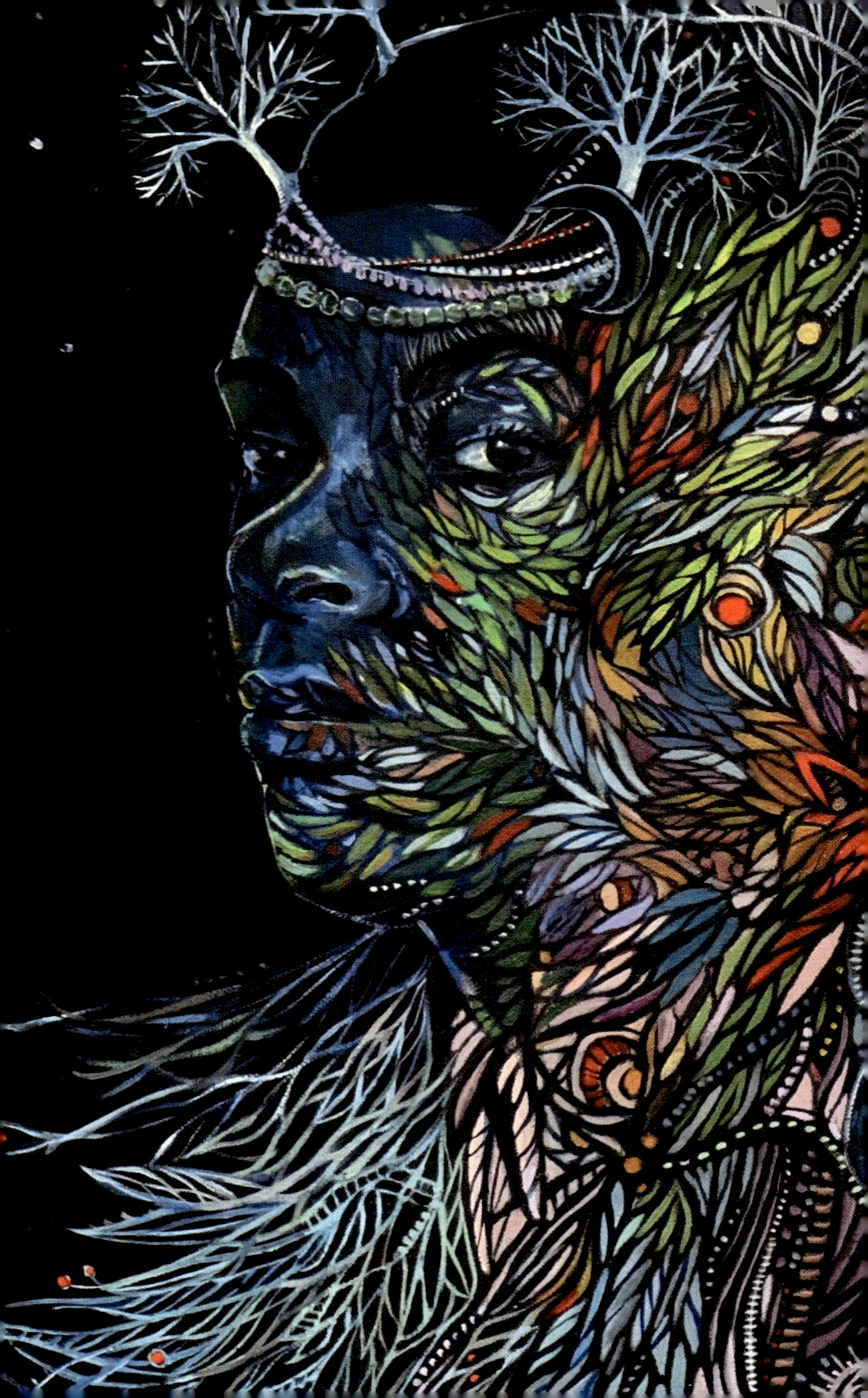

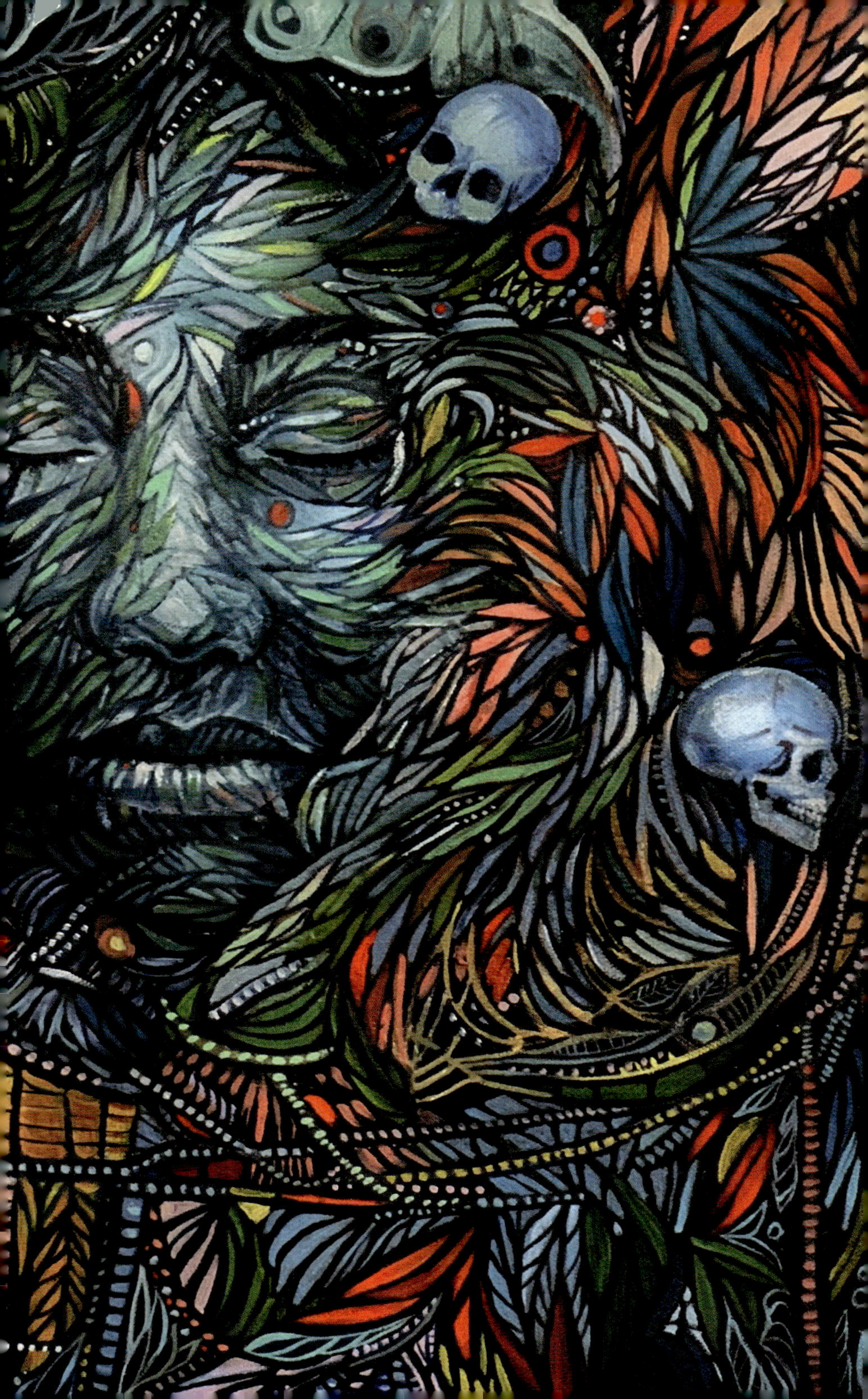

Our Skin

Sadness wraps itself gently around
pulls your shoulders forward in a half moon shape
to protect your heart from further pain
bows your head in reverence
at the fragility of life
watching the preciousness float by
delicate like a bubble that will pop to the touch
that will quickly evaporate into nothingness
nearly translucent, a thin rainbow barrier
the only thing that allows the eye to know
it exists at all

Joy pulls your shoulders
to open you like a star
lifts your head to see that yes, it is true
everything, everything floats by
preciously, fragilely, delicately
passing onward eventually
and yes it is pain and suffering and darkness
but there is eternal light that offers up
this miraculous tiny rainbow
on even the most insignificant
light
that is held within even
the sweetest little lifespans

And most certainly that same light
is within us all
and the colors
if we look to see
oh, all the colors
on our own beautiful skin

AFFIRMATION

I hold space for both joy and pain
recognize the delicate nature of life
continually bow to the light within us all
and carry reverence for this reflection
in my own beautiful skin

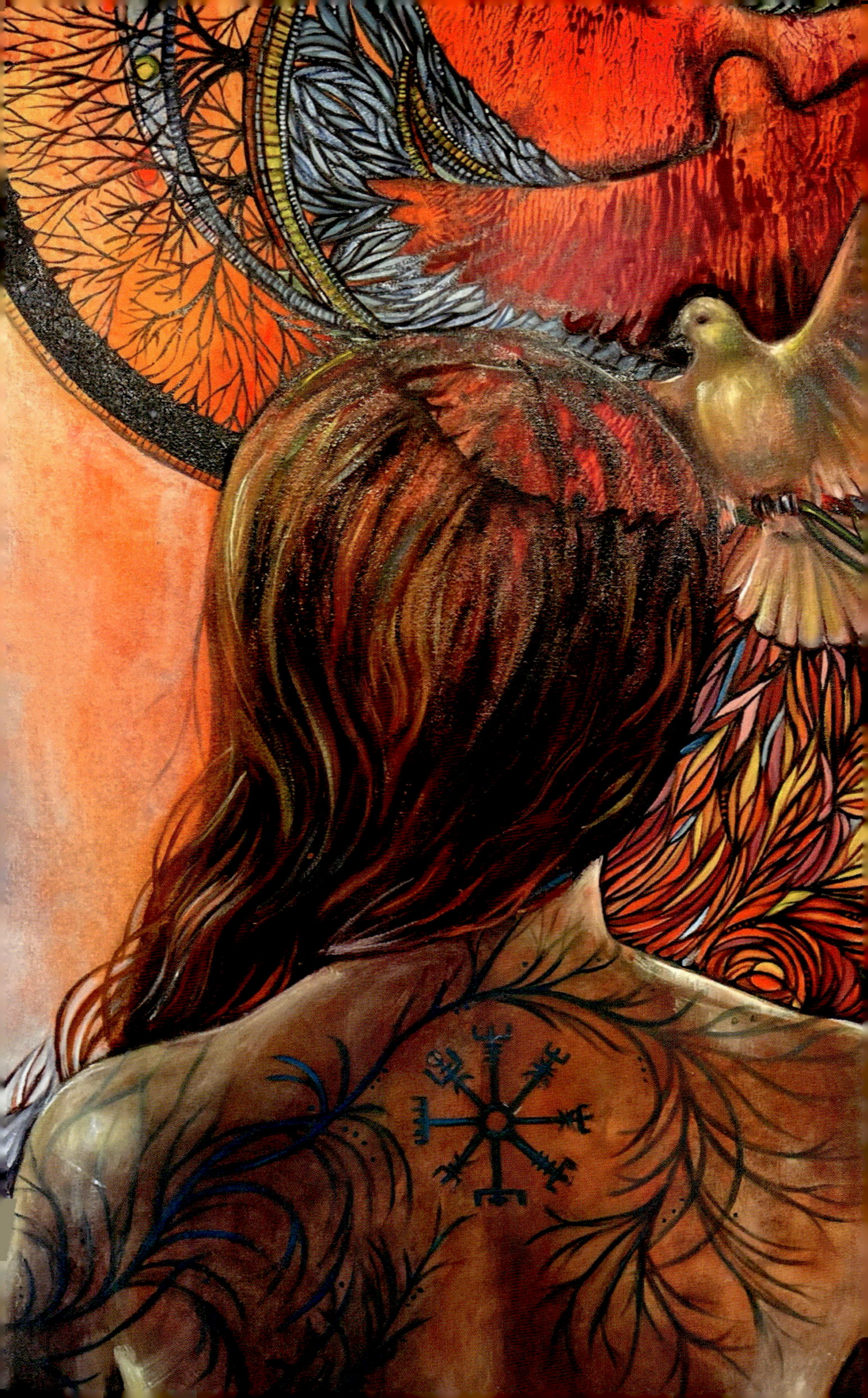

Radiant

I meet myself fully in the present moment exactly as I am

I lovingly embrace my whole-being, self-body-soul

I speak to and treat myself kindly and with utter compassion

I rest in my splendorous nature and live from my magnificence

I am radiant, this resonant Life Force hums through me

I am glittering opalescence, my life effervescent

AFFIRMATION

I am joyfully radiant and whole

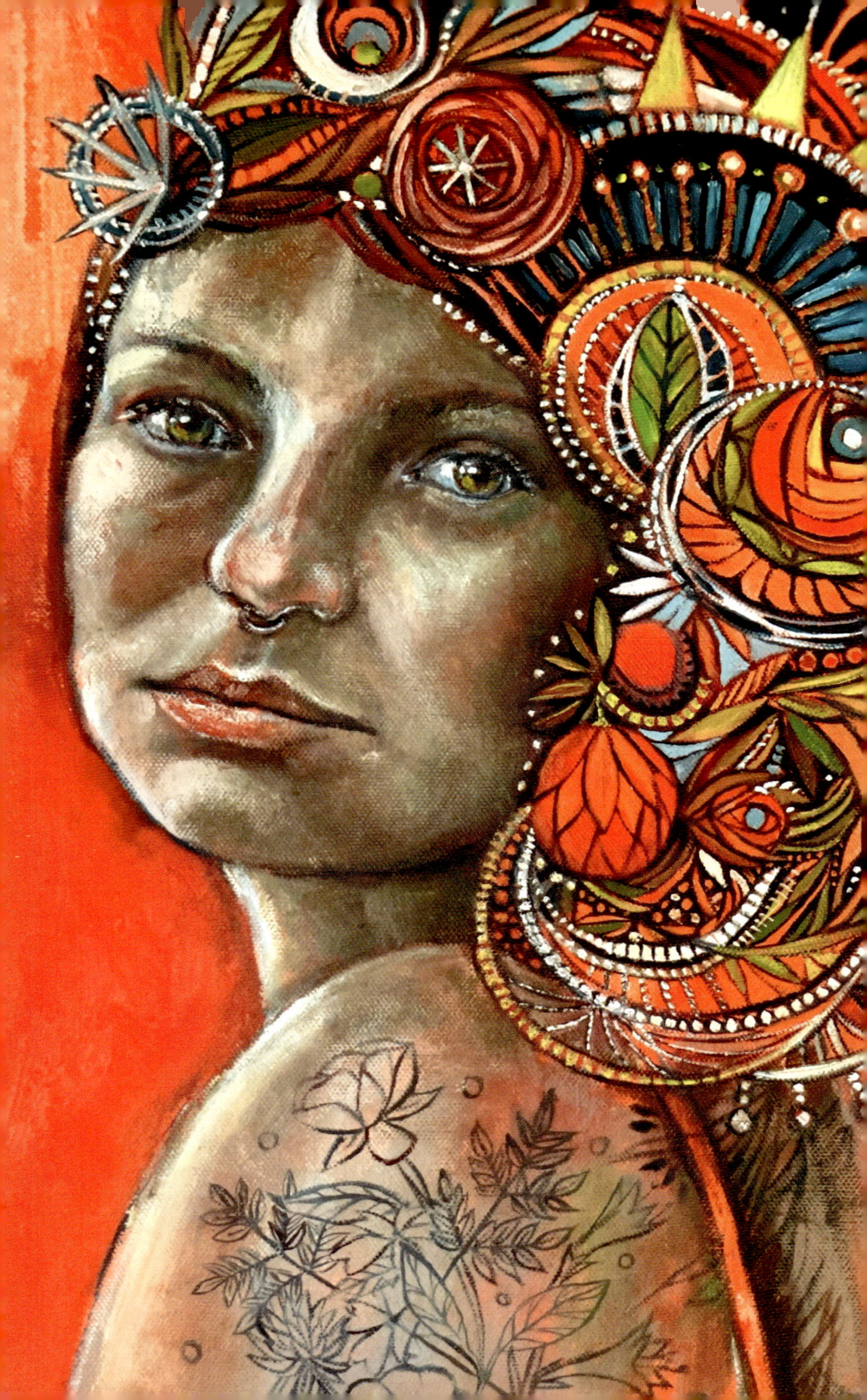

Receiving Blessings

What if you take them in
feel empty spaces in your heart
begin to fill
as if with helium
swelling with gratitude
until you are a sky inside
full of balloons in all colors floating
you count the many ways you are
loved, held, seen, cared for
the tiny joys, the kindnesses
(theirs/yours)
all floating within
lifting you up with invisible light

AFFIRMATION

I open space within to receive the blessings of my days
I recognize the ways I am loved, held, seen, and cared for
I intentionally take in the good and beautiful moments
I am filled with gratitude

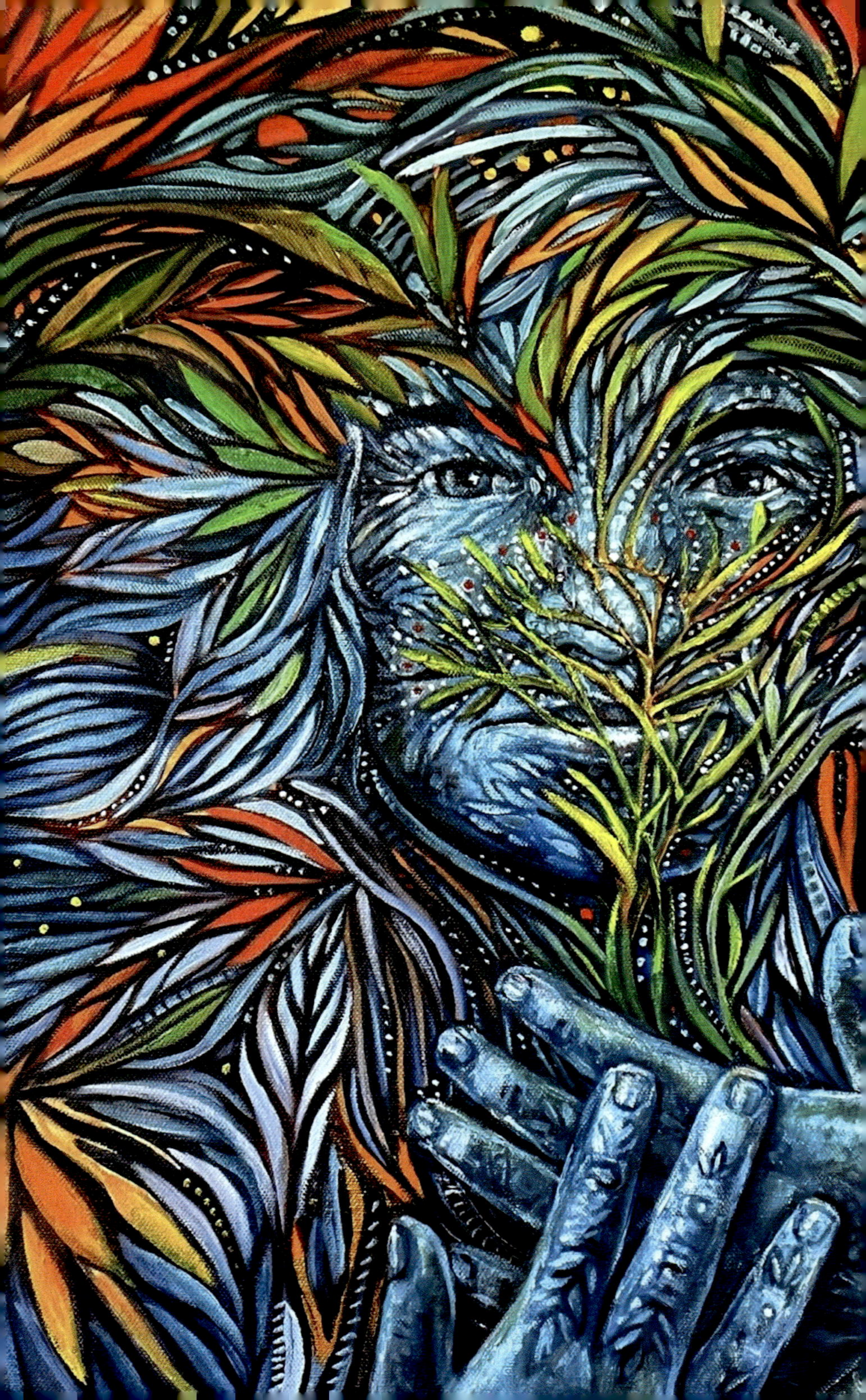

Resides Within

I am thirsty.

I don't realize I am already
overflowing with the
Source of Life.

This water swirls around all things.

Rushes into, undulates, pulls back,
pools inside,
resides.

AFFIRMATION

I already have everything I need
I reside within the Source of Life and
the Source of Life resides within me

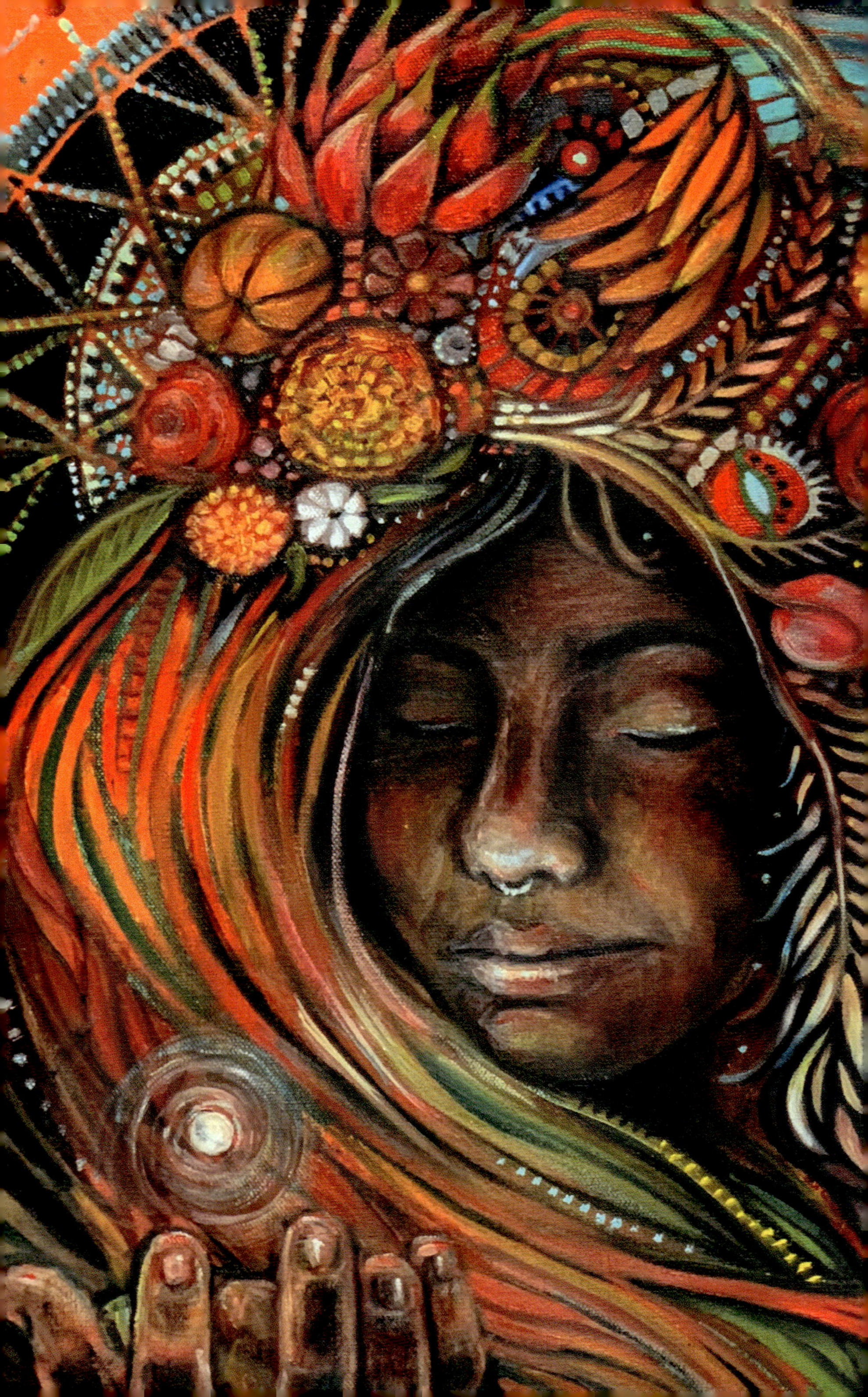

Reverence

I want to have a perpetual
sense of awe knocked into me
with the force of reverence
even this small slice
of honeydew melon deserves
luminous gentle green glow
(almost like a lightning bug)
bare, content, patient, and still
dewy as summer mornings
subtle sweetness on my lips
soft, tender, nourishing

How can I not utter
"thank you, thank you."
a million times over?

AFFIRMATION

I pay attention with awe to the nourishing
and good things life offers me daily
I receive pleasure
I take time to savor the sweetness of my life

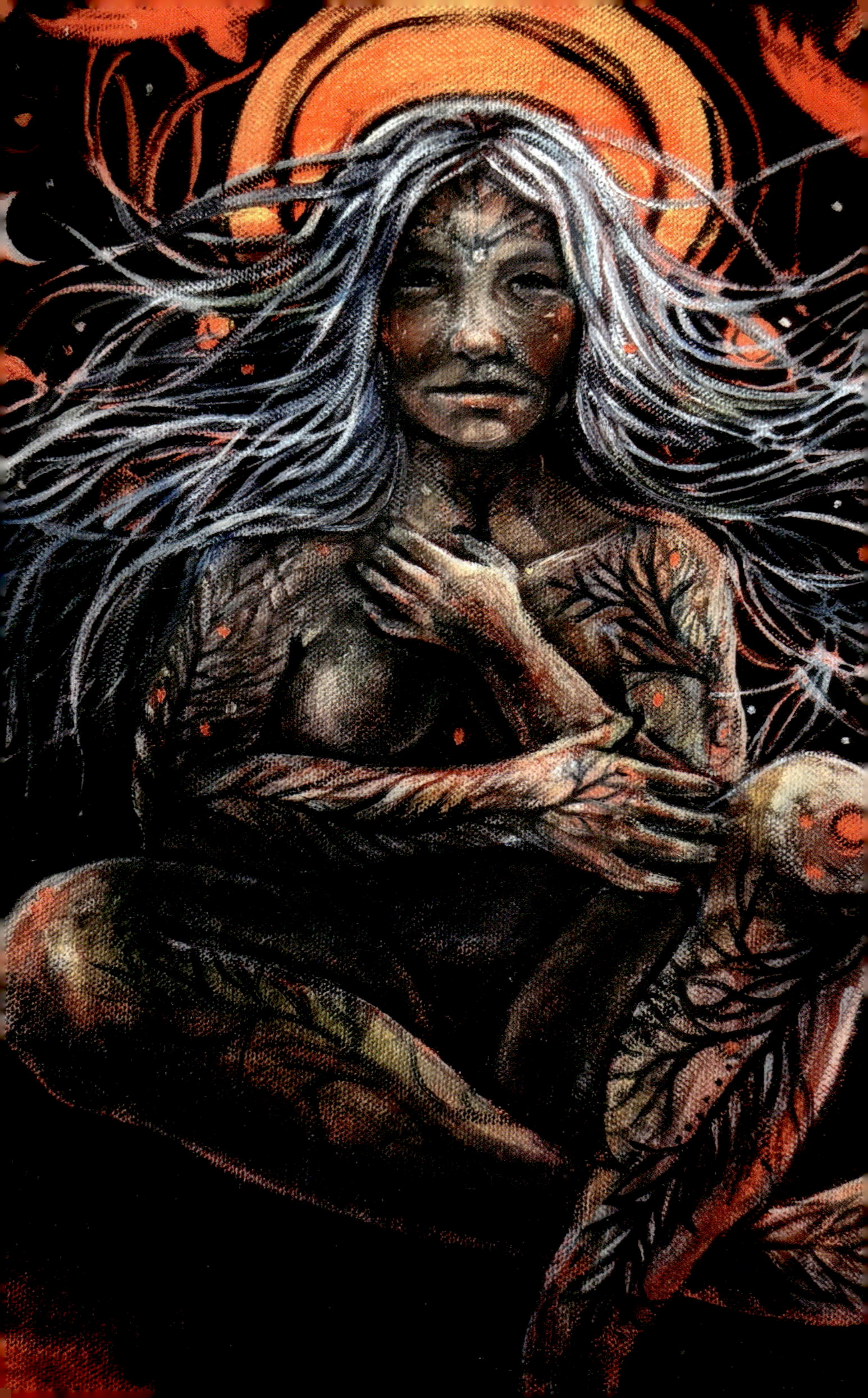

Revolution

I acknowledge that I emerged from a long line of great historical, spiritual, personal and collective trauma. No matter my position or privilege, I am touched and impacted by the whole. Equally, I touch and impact the whole. I pause to recognize that trauma runs through generations and is a part of the human condition—all of us carry our ancestral, collective, and personal stories and wounds.

I am grounded in the truth that we all hold within ourselves incredible ancestral, collective, and personal strength, resilience, and potential for healing, transformation, and growth—***for the most revolutionary act I can embark upon is my own healing***. Feeling the roots of this reach out from myself to the collective, sensing that we are all deeply connected, we are One, and together we can create a world where all people can belong and be whole. My presence and impact is powerful.

May I honor my wholeness, the unique and beautiful tapestry of me – all my shadows and light. For all I have been through has shaped me into who I am today. May I embrace darkness, pain, mistakes, and difficulties as profound offerings for growth and awakening. May I be rooted in Source and live from the place within of love, truth, peace, and wisdom. May I learn to bear all aspects of human existence with clarity and grace. May I approach my life as a laboratory and a grand opportunity to explore challenges and discomfort with more ease and to experience greater presence, peace, pleasure, and well-being. May this assist me in wise discernment to make skillful choices and take effective action to support my, and others', highest good. May this moment be blessed.

AFFIRMATION

My personal healing is a powerful revolutionary act

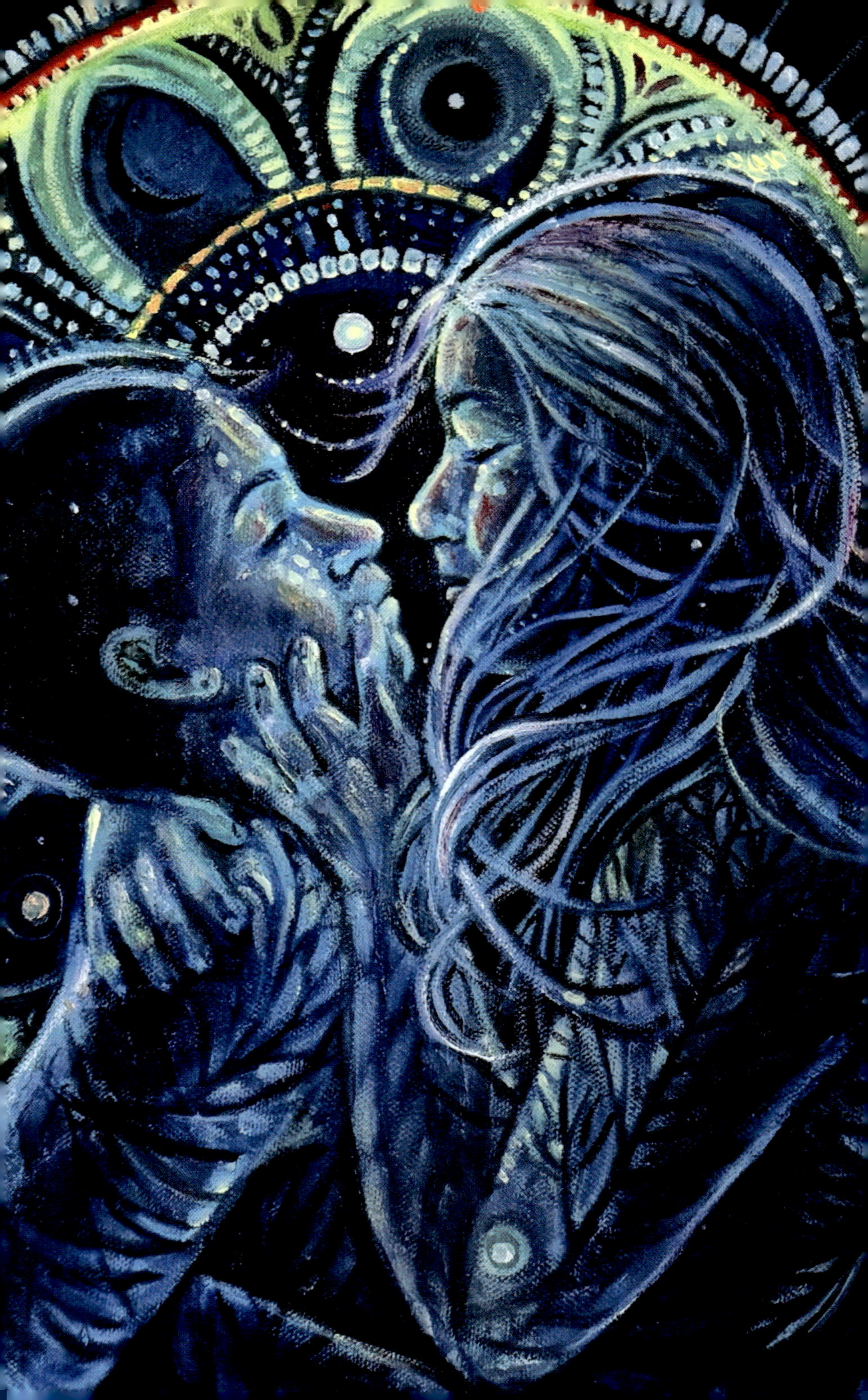

Shivering Sweetness

I taste earth, wetness
lick dew off a morning petal just opened
cool against my hot tongue
the rich smell of dank moss

We are fire
flicker, unfurl
throw sparks as we dance
tremble
drums humming, maracas shaking

Our lips shine with melted butter
with the grit of sugar dripping down our chins

We sway and our song bellows
there is the ache of love swelling
swooning up from the deepest places inside of us
an ancient unfurling, singing the original song of creation

For a moment everything becomes nothing
suspended on air, pollen floating
white, weightless, translucent
in waves undulating, softly
gently rising, falling
until we land on earth, on water
steady
received tenderly

AFFIRMATION

I am a vibrant, alive, and sensual being
I meet my life fully through my incredible senses
I receive and savor the sweetness available to me

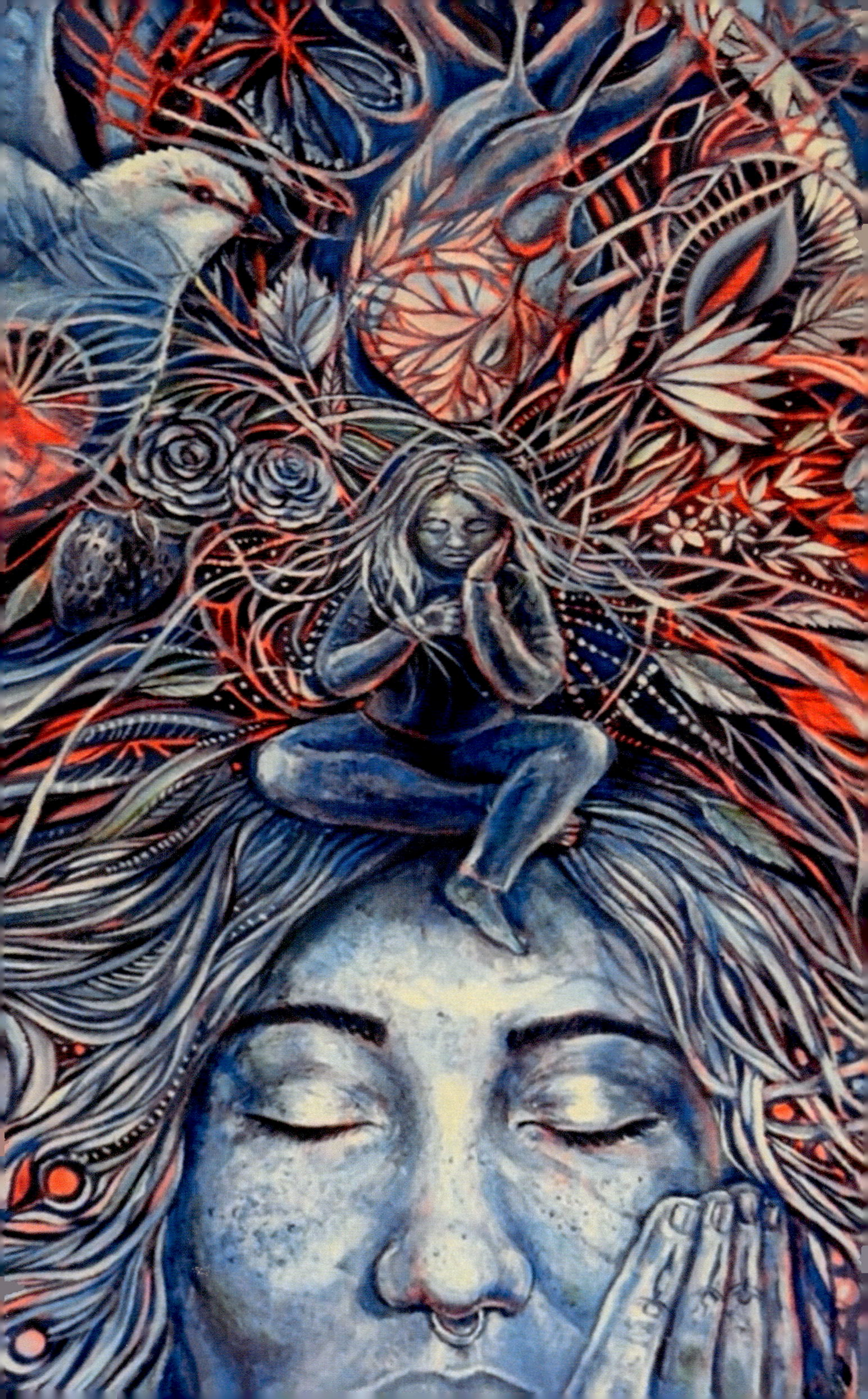

Sitting with Myself

This human experience
we try to hold as if a bucket
fill with memories of once

Yet we cannot contain, elusive
it overflows with the moments we live

Yet there is a foreverness
the way it all shapes who we are
(becoming, becoming)
and how we tend to this precious plot of life we are given
is everything, everything
can I be the tenderest imaginable with seeds and soil I'm given
with every tiny and great wreckage and wound
and especially, especially
with each unfurling bit of beauty that rises up
through phases and seasons, blossoms and decay
how can I not honor both the gouges and miracles of living
and whisper to each divine one
I love you. Thank you.

AFFIRMATION

I honor both the gouges and miracles of living with tenderness
I whisper to each divine one
I love you. Thank you.

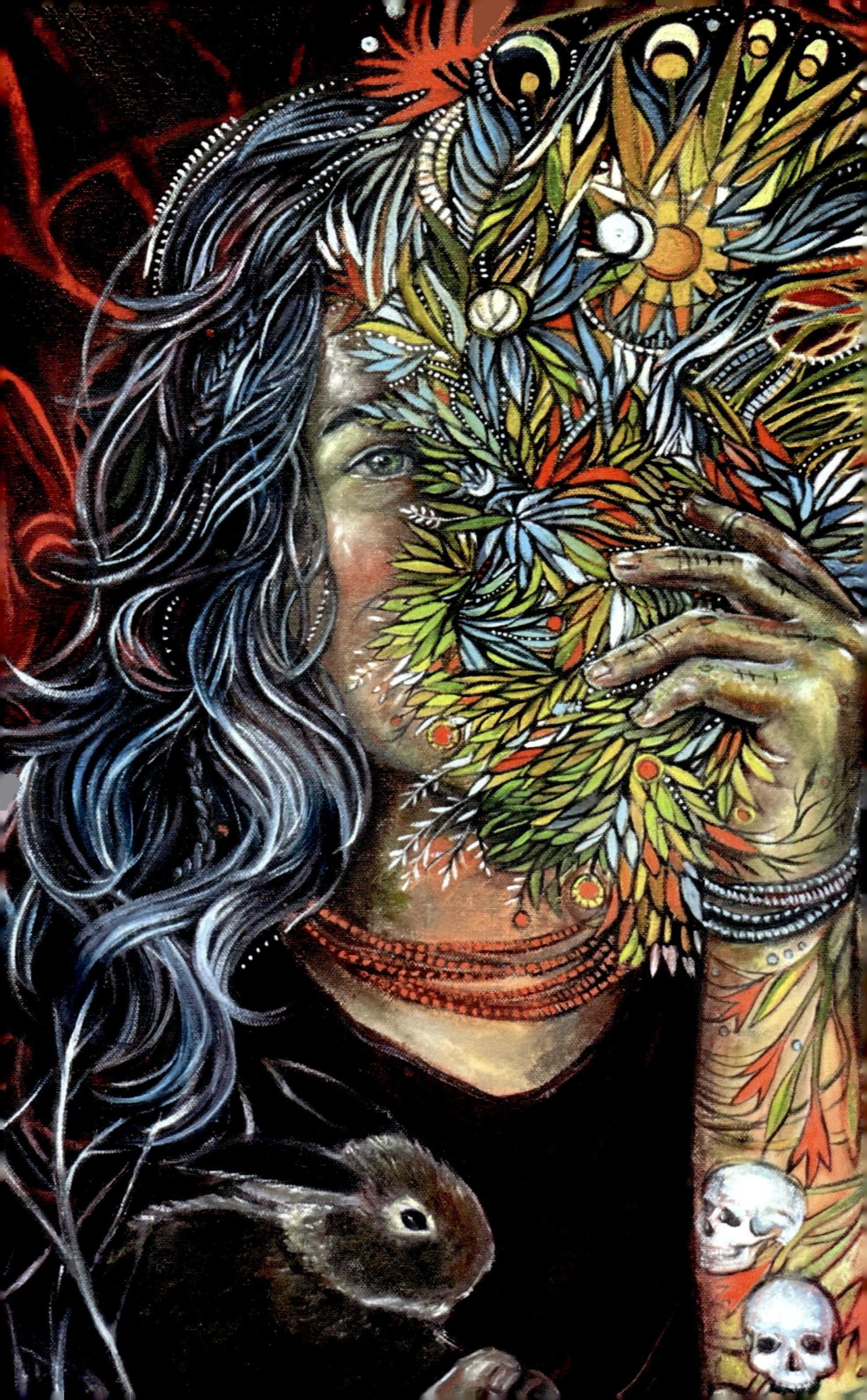

Sky in Our Eyes

Lying outside on the grass, earth holds me
my body a prayer, an offering
of every beautiful and terrible thing
it has endured, lived, celebrated, survived

Gratitude swells
for all the ways my body has carried me
to this ordinary miraculous moment

Each experience a trap door to new worlds
places inside me I never knew existed

We aren't here to stay safe
in only one room, to cling only to joy
mirages of the moments we loved most
the illusion that anything can last forever

We cannot bow forever at each of these losses
cannot hold vigil to this pain indefinitely
sometimes it is time to blow out the candles we lit
we carry it, hold it all
place every single one in a cemetery in our hearts
we did not know these stones crack open
reveal precious glowing gemstones
in kaleidoscope colors within us

We are here to experience vast landscapes
wider and wilder than our imagination
fields of vibrant untamed wildflowers
bopping their tender heads, as if at a concert
this music is constantly playing, humming for us all
if we pause and look up, we realize we all hold the entire sky
reflected in our own eyes

AFFIRMATION

I thank my body for the way it has carried me throughout my life
I hold and honor all my experiences indiscriminately, beautiful and terrible
I release my human tendency to cling only to the good and dwell on my pain
I step into the vastness of my life and trust in my continued awakening

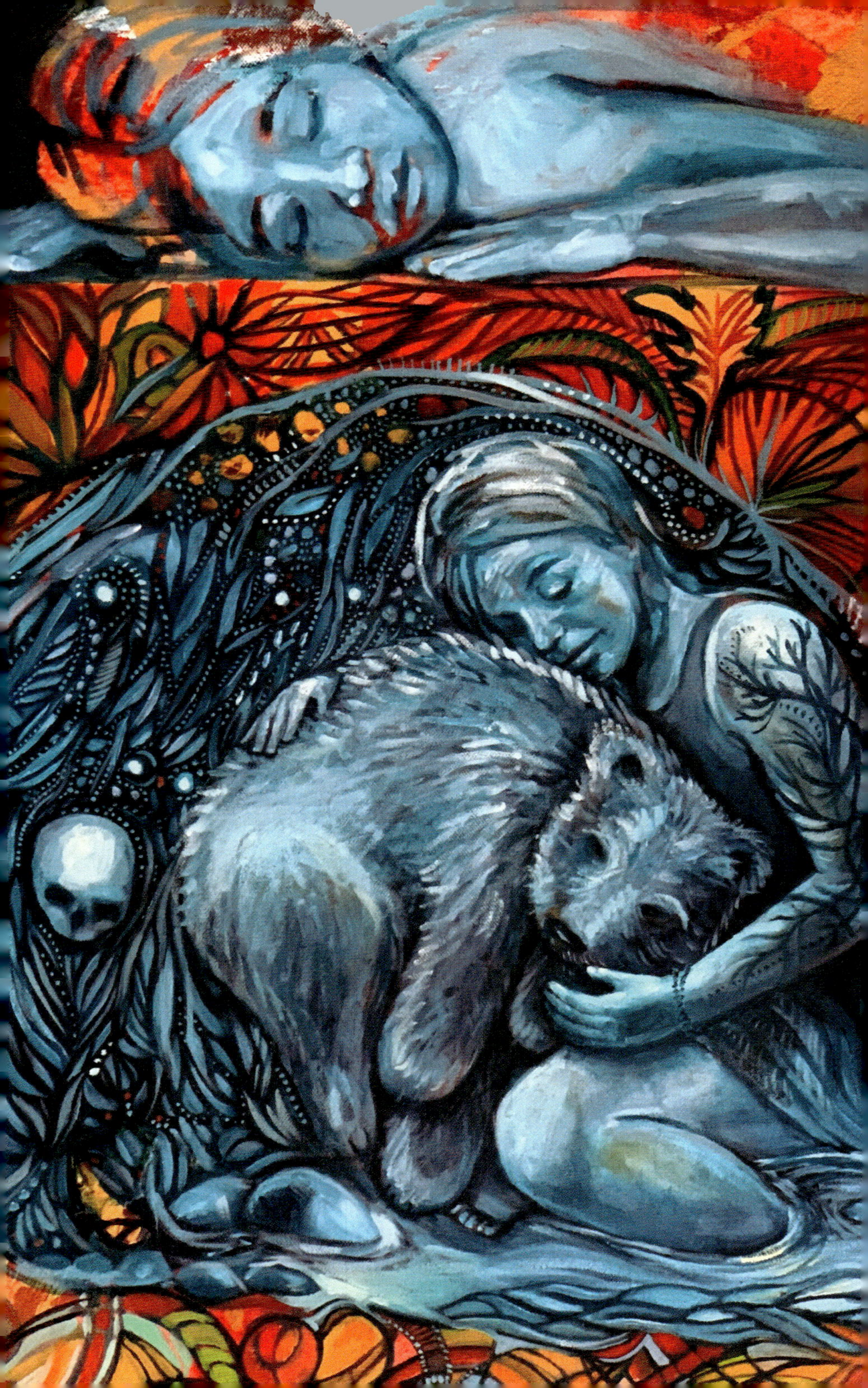

Sorrow

Sometimes we have a sorrow
that is so painful
in the deep of winter
the dark season of our loss
as a bear hibernates to survive
this sorrow retreats
tucks herself sweetly
safely away
into the crevices of our being
as long as she needs

Eventually finding her way
to the thaw
the cracking
the breaking open of ice
the rivers of our pain
rushing beneath
f r e e d
a call to what
is wild in us

When we are ready and able
to be with our sorrow
she reappears
longing for the tender touch
of sunshine
the sweet songs of spring
awakening the love
resting at the center of our loss
and she crawls out of her cave
announcing her existence
unleashing resonate
primordial cries of
a l i v e n e s s

AFFIRMATION

I am present with the unfolding seasons of my sorrow
I tend gently to the natural rhythms and unfurling wisdom of grief

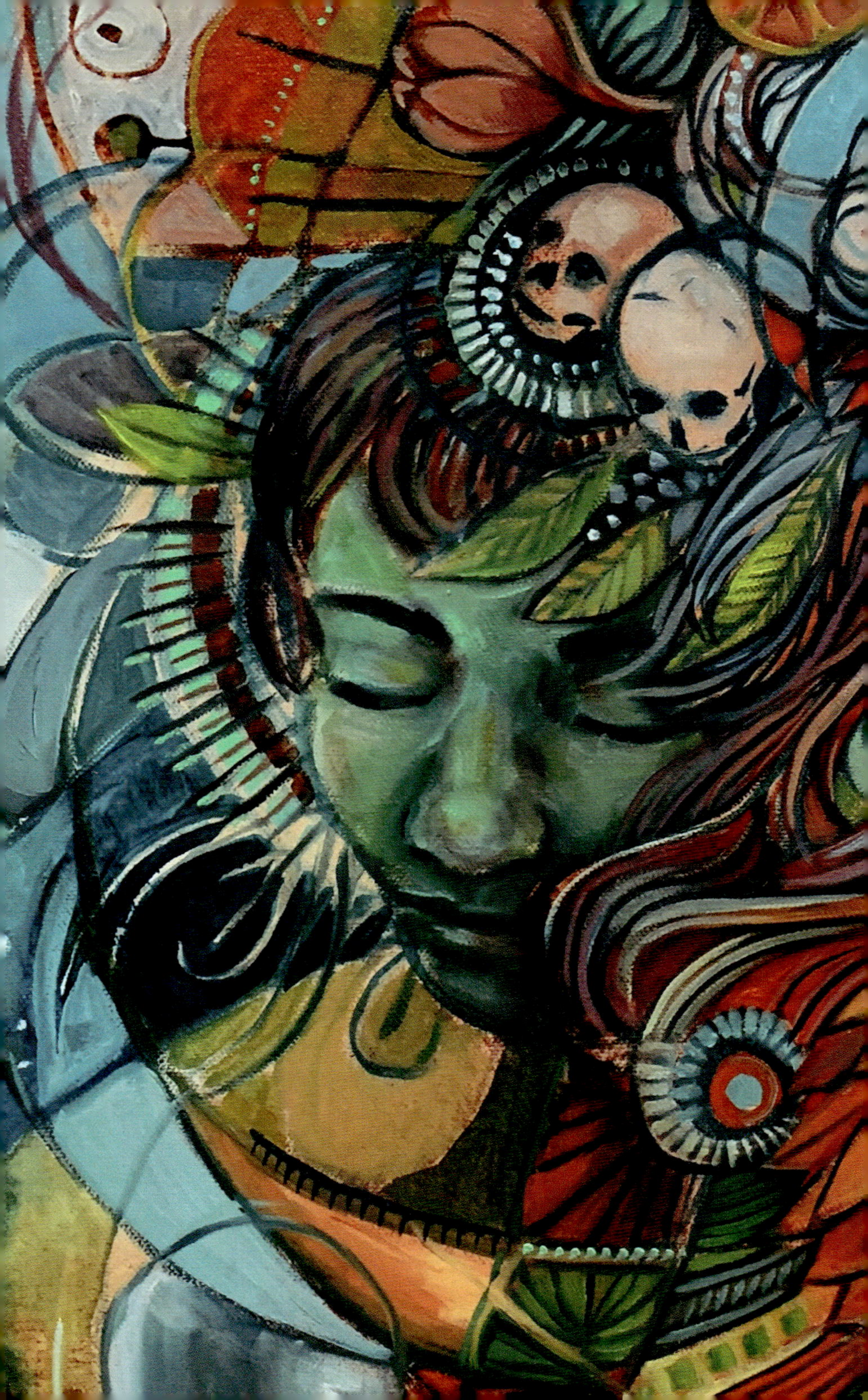

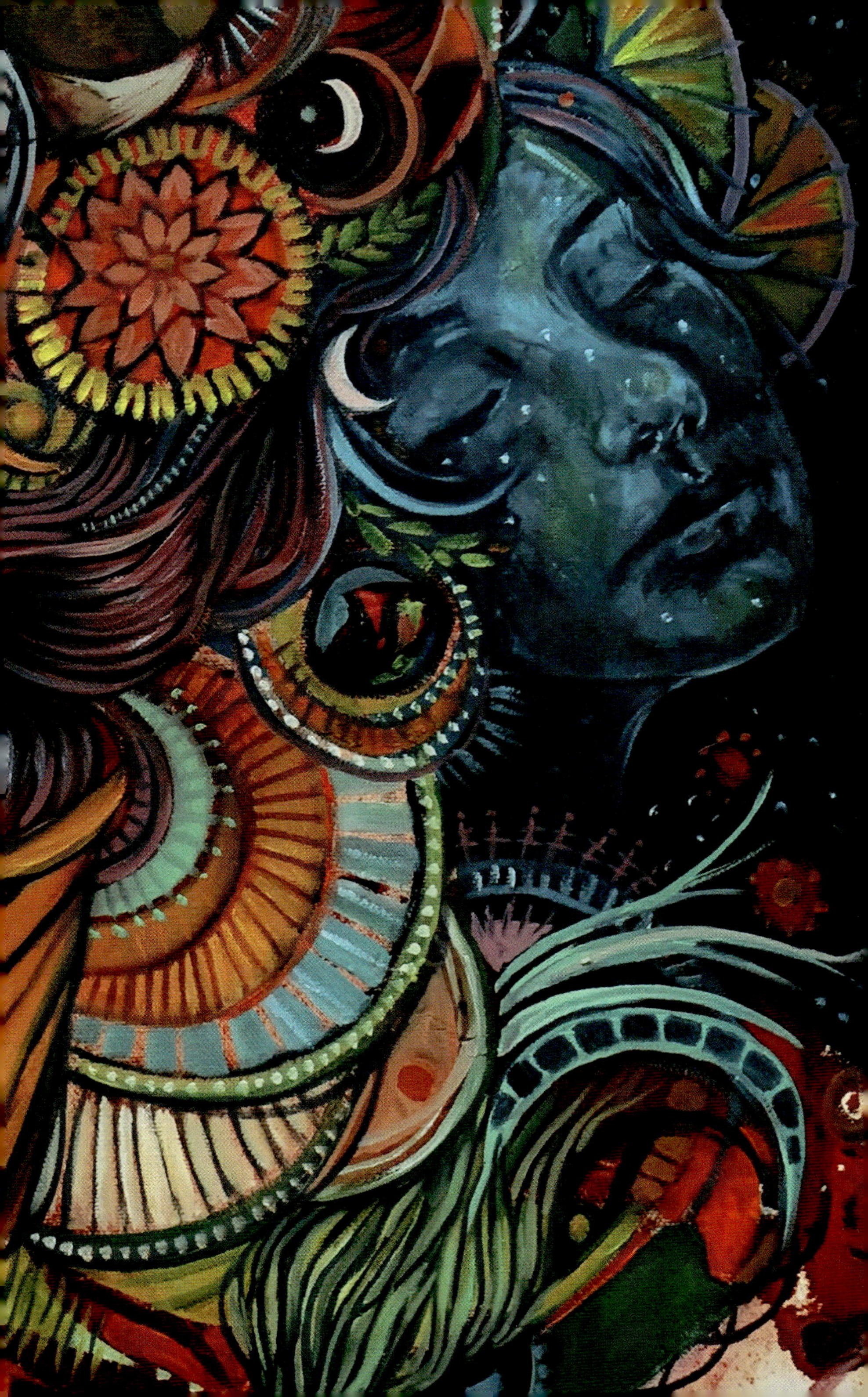

Spinning Gold

May I be with the inevitable suffering of life with more ease and peace

May I mindfully reduce the unnecessary suffering I cause myself and others

May I open to the sweetness, joy, and pleasure life generously offers even in dark and difficult moments

May I connect with mySelf and be anchored in the belonging of Home within, my inner-sanctuary

May I know my innate wholeness, worth, and enoughness - understanding that all is welcome, everything belongs, joy and pain, happiness and sorrow, mistakes and successes, for all I have been through has shaped me into who I am today

May I learn to listen to my inner-knowing and take effective action to respond skillfully to the circumstances of my life and this world

May I make the positive changes that are possible for me and contribute to the highest good for myself and others

May everything that arises be cultivated for my continued evolution and awakening

May I welcome the healing that is possible and make meaning from valuable lessons at the center of all I am given

May I realize I hold the magic of the Spinner in my own fingertips and gently guide the fibers of my experiences through this great Wheel of Life, spinning, spinning, spun until transformed into the gorgeous gold threads of my sacred existence

AFFIRMATION

I hold the magic of the Spinner within
I gently guide the fibers of my experience
spinning, transforming, spun
into gorgeous gold threads
of my sacred existence

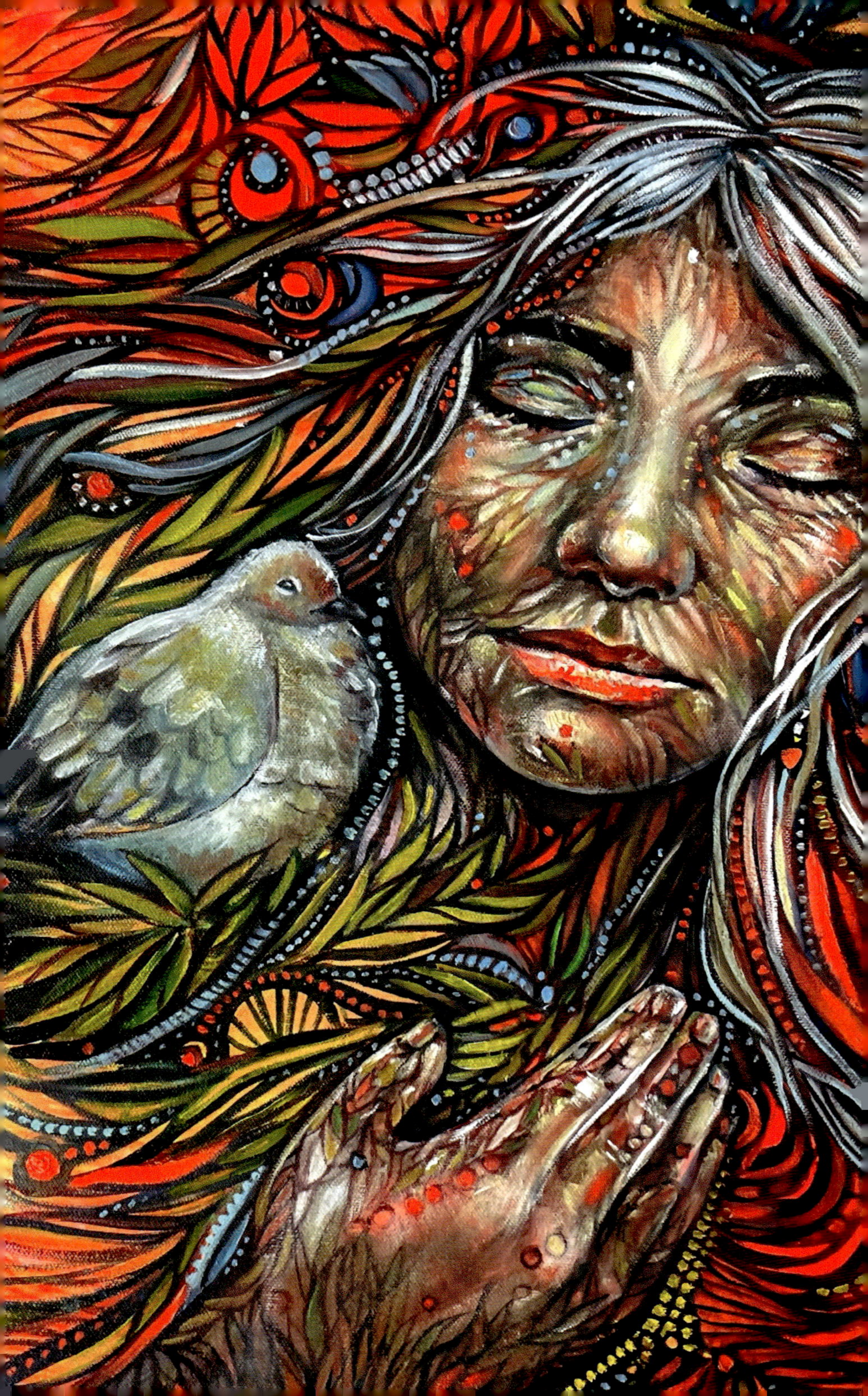

Stained Glass Reflection

Your body, your being is a wonder
a vast landscape
a vibrant collection of pieces and parts
of all that has happened
all you have experienced
survived

A mosaic placed together just so
telling the story of you
and no matter the colors
the strange and sometimes jagged
shapes and configurations of your life
the fragments and what feels like broken pieces
within the masterpiece
in the chapel of your existence
if you step back with just a little distance
you will stand in nothing but awe
at the miraculous stained glass reflection of yourself
and the stunning way the light always, always filters through

AFFIRMATION

I see fully the wholeness of my life
I am in awe of the gorgeous stained glass mosaic
of my miraculous existence

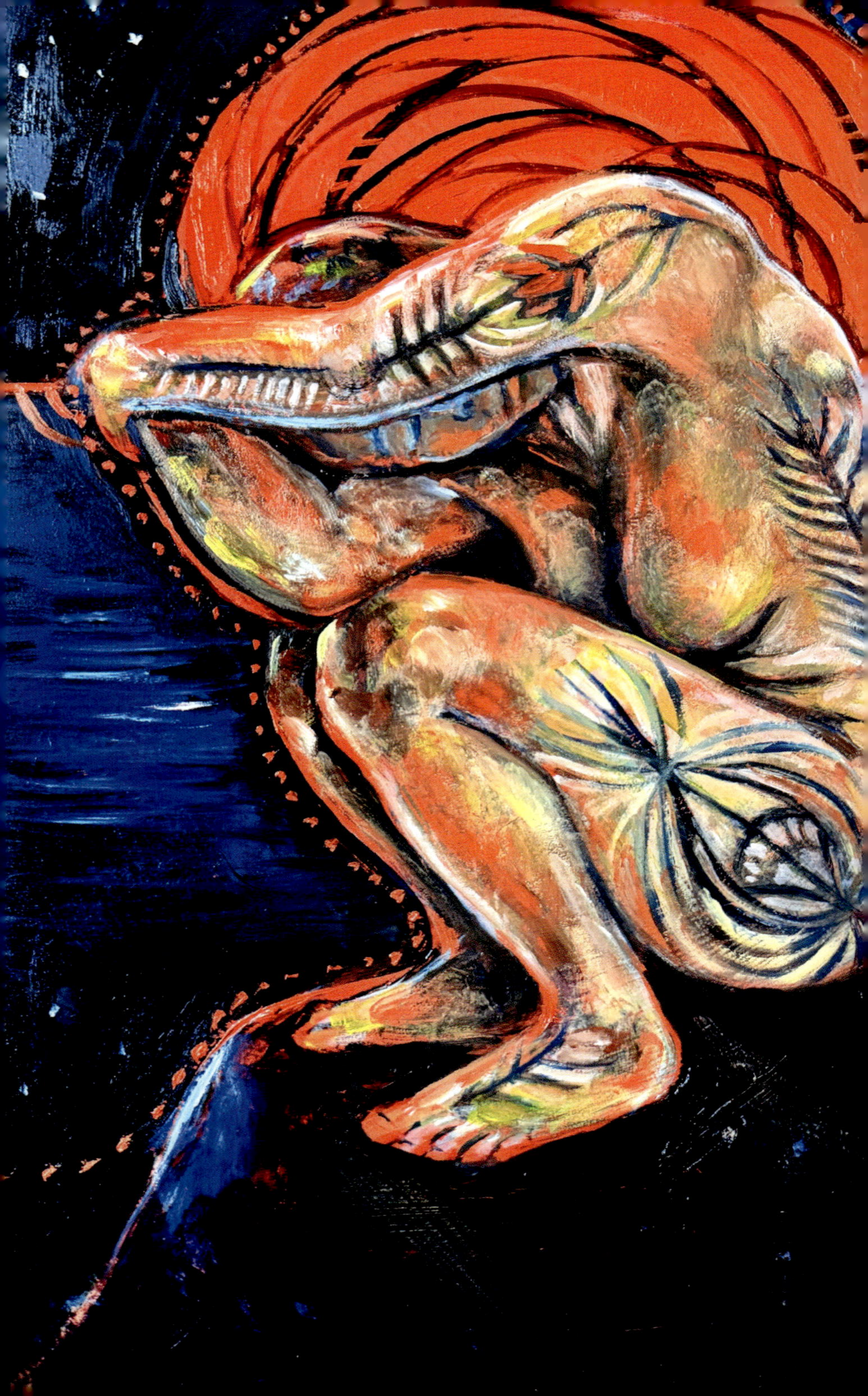

Strength

Every time you think,
"I cannot take any more!"
and want to give up
watch this doubt dissolve
against your strength
Because you are a warrior
look at all you have
survived
(strong beyond measure)

AFFIRMATION

I am strong beyond measure

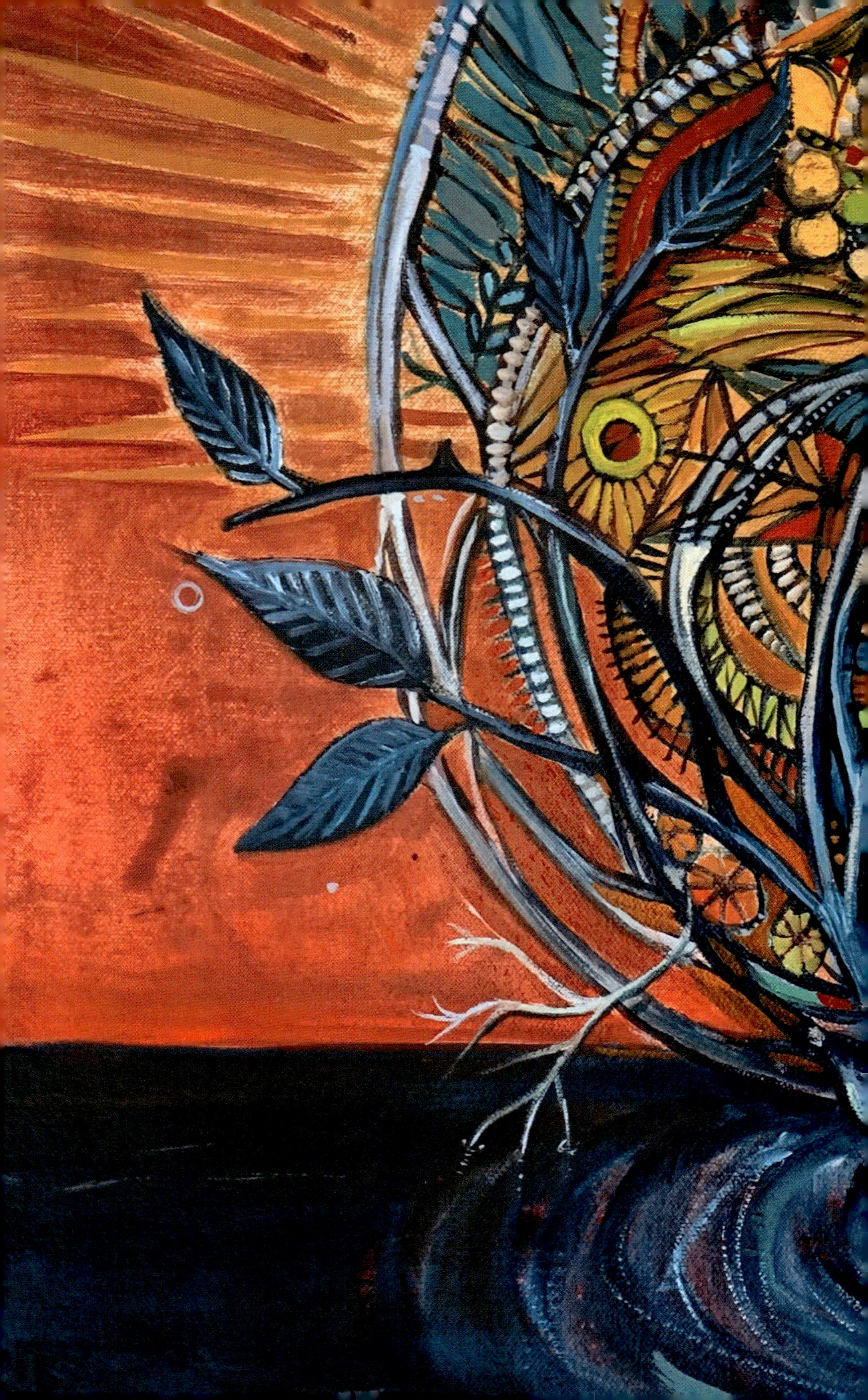

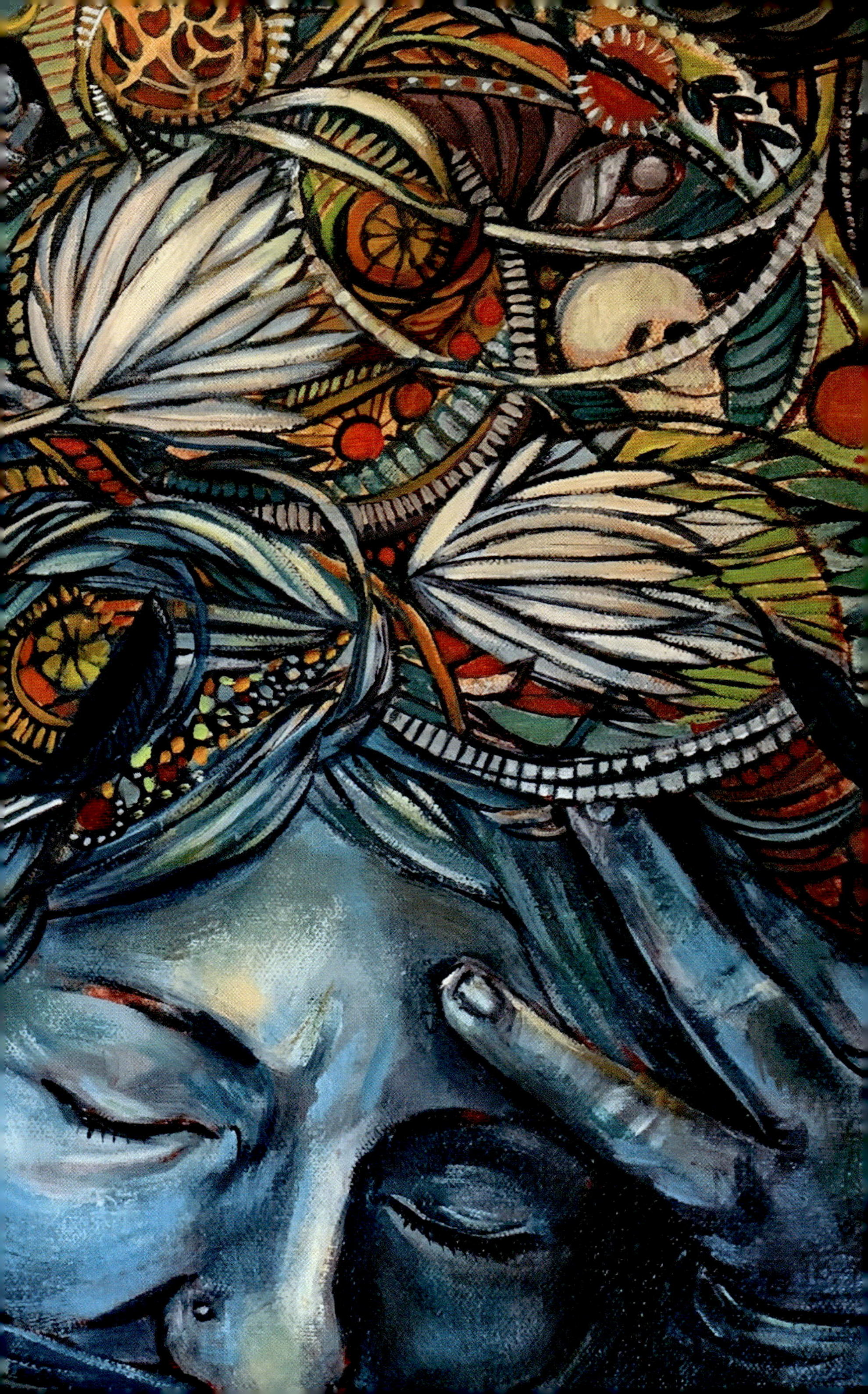

Supermoon

When there are no words
for things this difficult and devastating,
there are no words
tonight
the Supermoon rises.

There are no words,
but in the silence,
as the light we may know,
or have hoped for,
the light we are grasping for
like an ancient name on the
tip of our tongue we've forgotten,
but know in the deepest way
still strain to remember
the daylight slips through
fingers like water we cannot hold.

There are no words to describe,
language for this does not exist
so we strain and close our eyes,
forehead in hands,
pulling at our own hair
and face the impending darkness.

When there are no words
tonight this moon rises
shows us a power beyond comprehension,
a light larger than imaginable,
that has not been this big,
this bright, this close for 68 years
transmutes the night pushing aside our fear
light rolling out of the mouth of darkness
uttering those words, the million names for the Beloved
on our lips that press against this earth, beautifully exposed
the body of this world undressed for you
all the edges and lines urging you
to touch.

AFFIRMATION

Especially in darkness, when there are no words for such pain or horror
I cultivate the power of the Supermoon,
connect with a strength beyond comprehension
and a light larger than imaginable
I still see the beauty on this earth and in my life
urging me to touch and make contact with what is sacred, even so

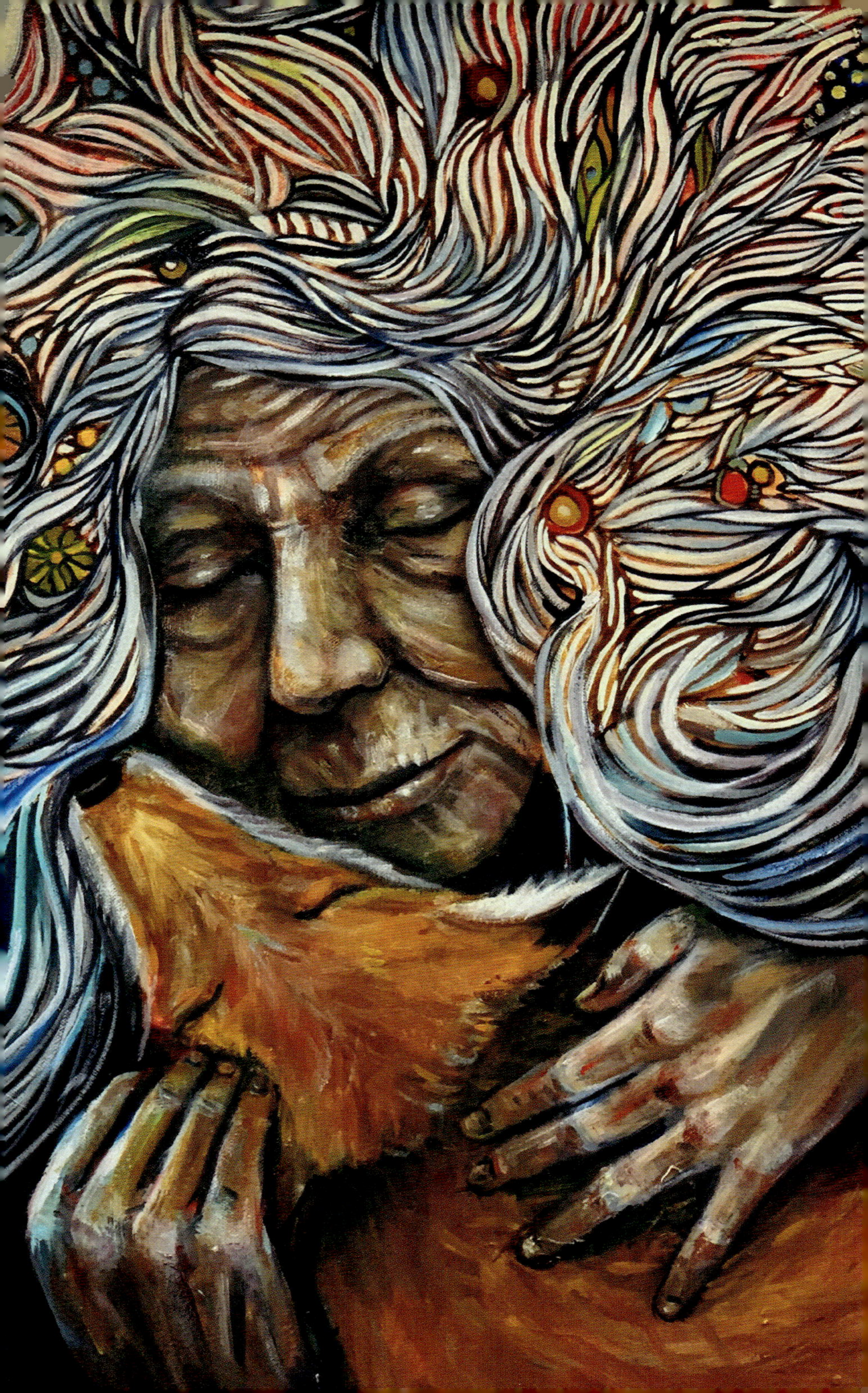

The Grandmother of the World

A single song
can floor you then lift you up
as if by strings
until you levitate
and know you are held
(never alone)
in an invisible
Ocean of Love

A walk through the woods
steady footsteps
a metronome
a sway back and forth
rewiring your brain
for what is good and beautiful
rocking in great Mama's arms
the sunlight funneling through trees
drawing delicate lace patterns
on everything she touches
the thick sturdy
dark brown bark of trees
rough against your hands
the smell of lake, of pine
of bonfire smoke

AFFIRMATION

I am held in an invisible ocean of Love, never alone
I am open and venture into the world to notice and receive
tiny miraculous moments everywhere

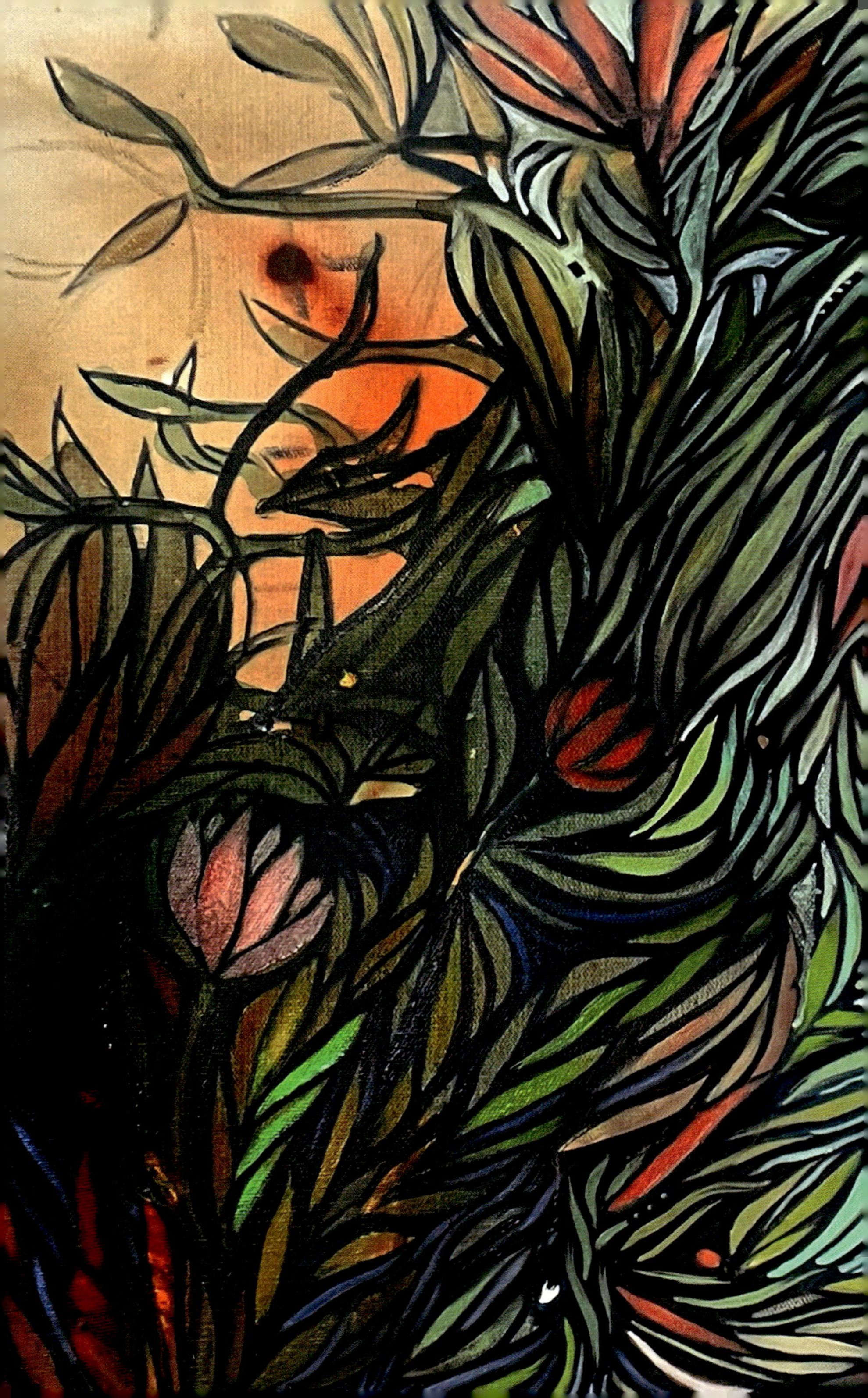

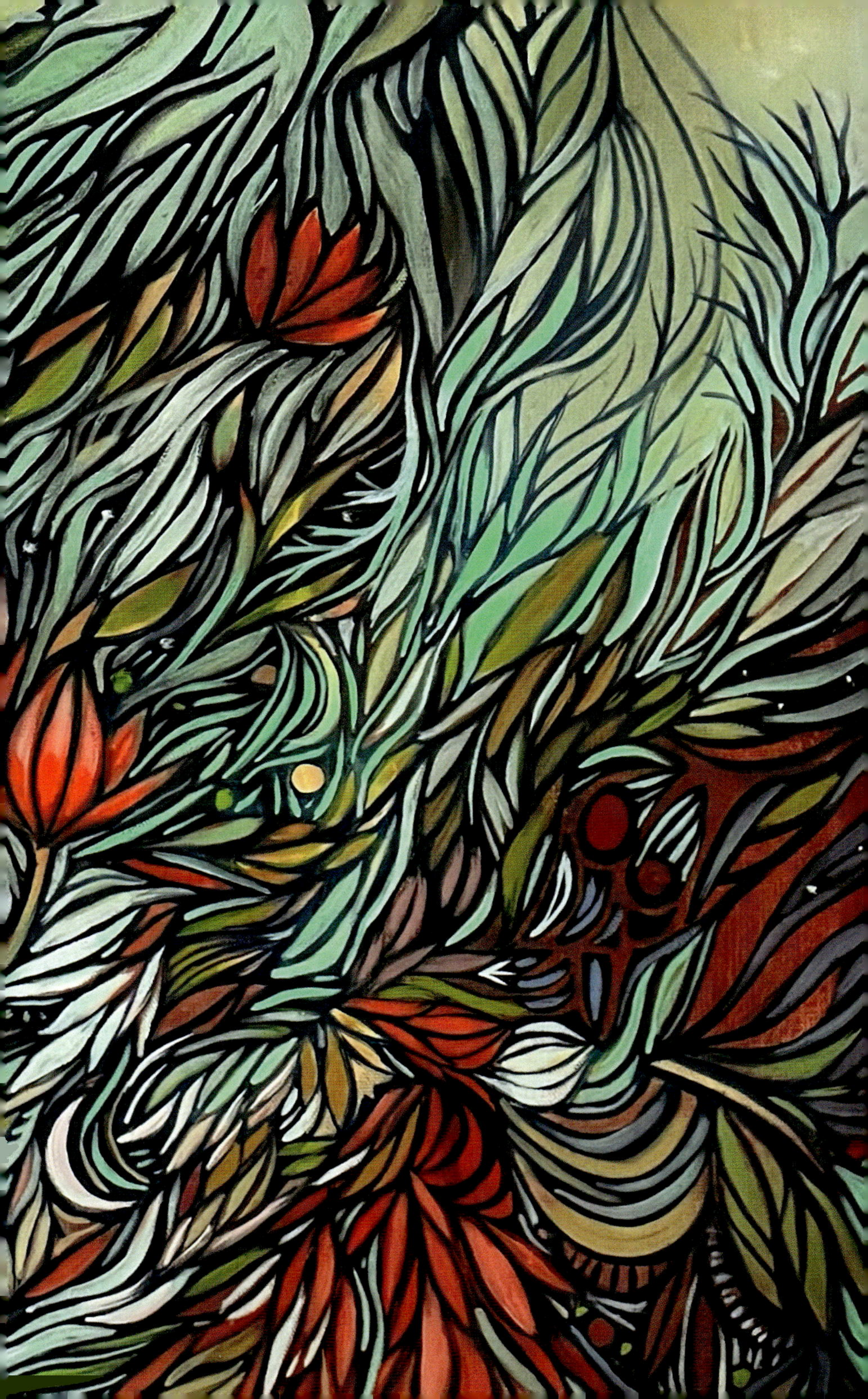

The Opening

Take the pistachio
its hard shell
that may break your teeth
if you try to eat it whole

Ravenous to be fed
you will not receive
what you seek
hungry for relief from your anguish
you will suffer more this way
some things just hurt
difficulty
cannot be something other
than what it is

Instead
be with your pain
observe the sorrows of life
with curiosity
roll the nut around
across your fingers
appreciating its milky color
feeling the smooth
way this protective armor
has formed around
its heart
until you notice the crack
the opening
carefully pull it apart
until a soft green, nearly glowing
seed is exposed
offering nourishment
in a form you can take in

Always there
within your pain
completely yours
to savor

AFFIRMATION

I meet the suffering of life with curiosity
I release my impulse to force relief from pain
I bear witness to the difficulties
I allow the stark reality to be exactly what it is
until the meaning opens, the pearl of wisdom revealed

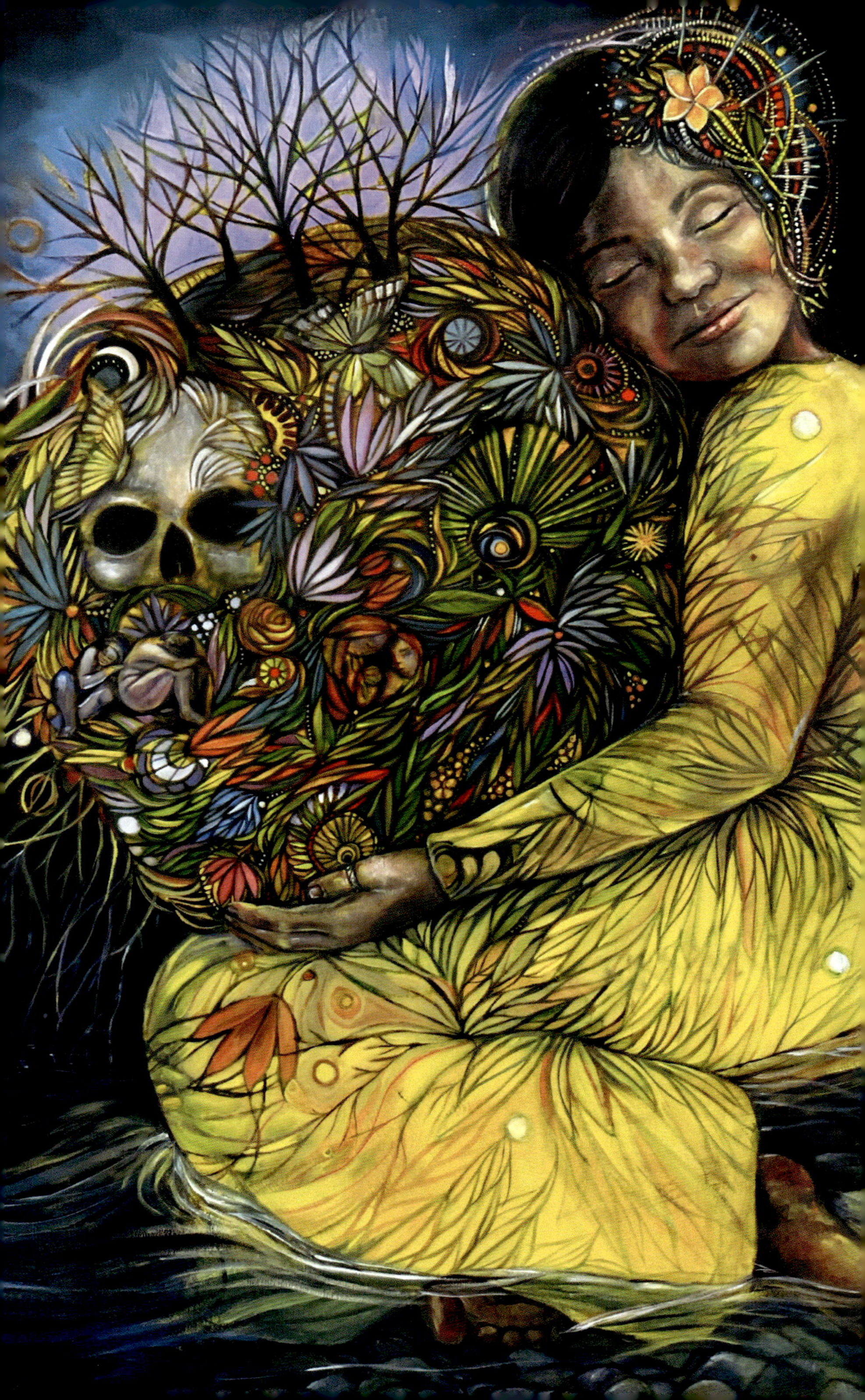

To Hold It All

Yes we carry it all
as a bird, its own feathers
every one received, needed to fly

As a tree, each ring spirals from its center
telling the story of your life
what happened, where and when
the delicate lines drawn
one inside another inside another inside another.

Here a joy, there denotes a sorrow
this knot smudged here, a dark cavern of pain
these spaces are filled with love
the intelligence of silvery silky birch bark
to softly protect, continually renewed
from strength within.

You are made to withstand
to hold it all
at first we think we cannot
then we expand
stretch in miraculous ways
we never imagined.

AFFIRMATION

I am capable, strong, and powerful enough
to expand and hold all I am given
I trust my inner-knowing to discern what is mine to hold,
when to say no, and when to let go

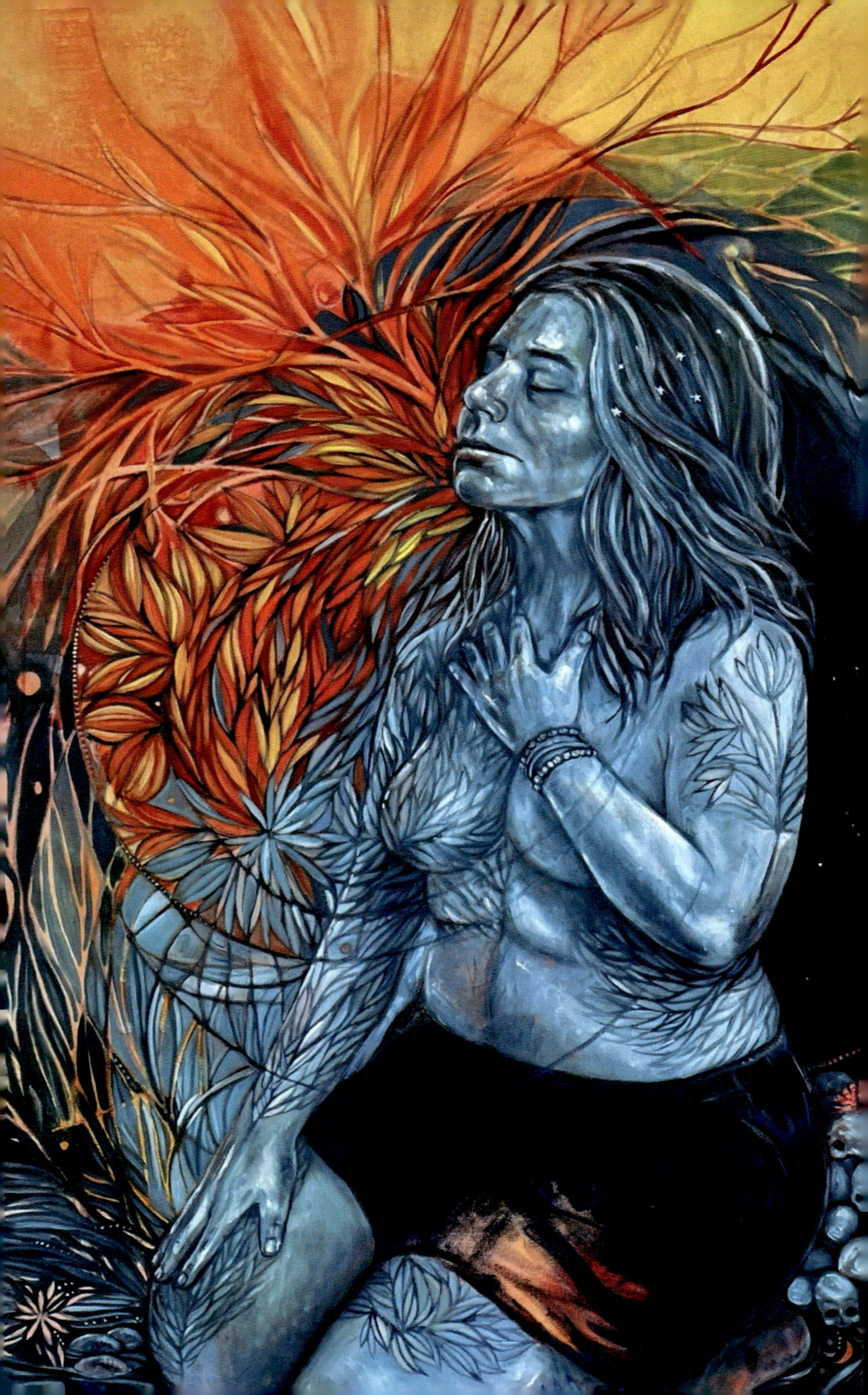

Transformational Fires of Pain

Grief, upon grief, upon grief
transform through the
fires of your pain

From traumatic losses that absolutely gut you, to small and large wounds or changes, even if they are good, grief is a part of life. Grief is a natural, beautiful, and human response that is inextricably connected to love. Yet it can feel overwhelming (unbearable) to be with our pain. Like a hand to a flame, our instinct is to pull away and do all we can to extinguish it. We frantically try to get rid of our pain through repression, banishment, numbing, or sideways rage we may blow through others. But, it is only through allowing the burning, by inviting our pain to rise into its fullness, that we can be transformed. Grief is powerful alchemy if we can open ourselves and create space for the magic to unfurl. This supports our awakening. We can do this with our own compassionate presence and that of our community.

AFFIRMATION

I am transformed through the fires of my pain

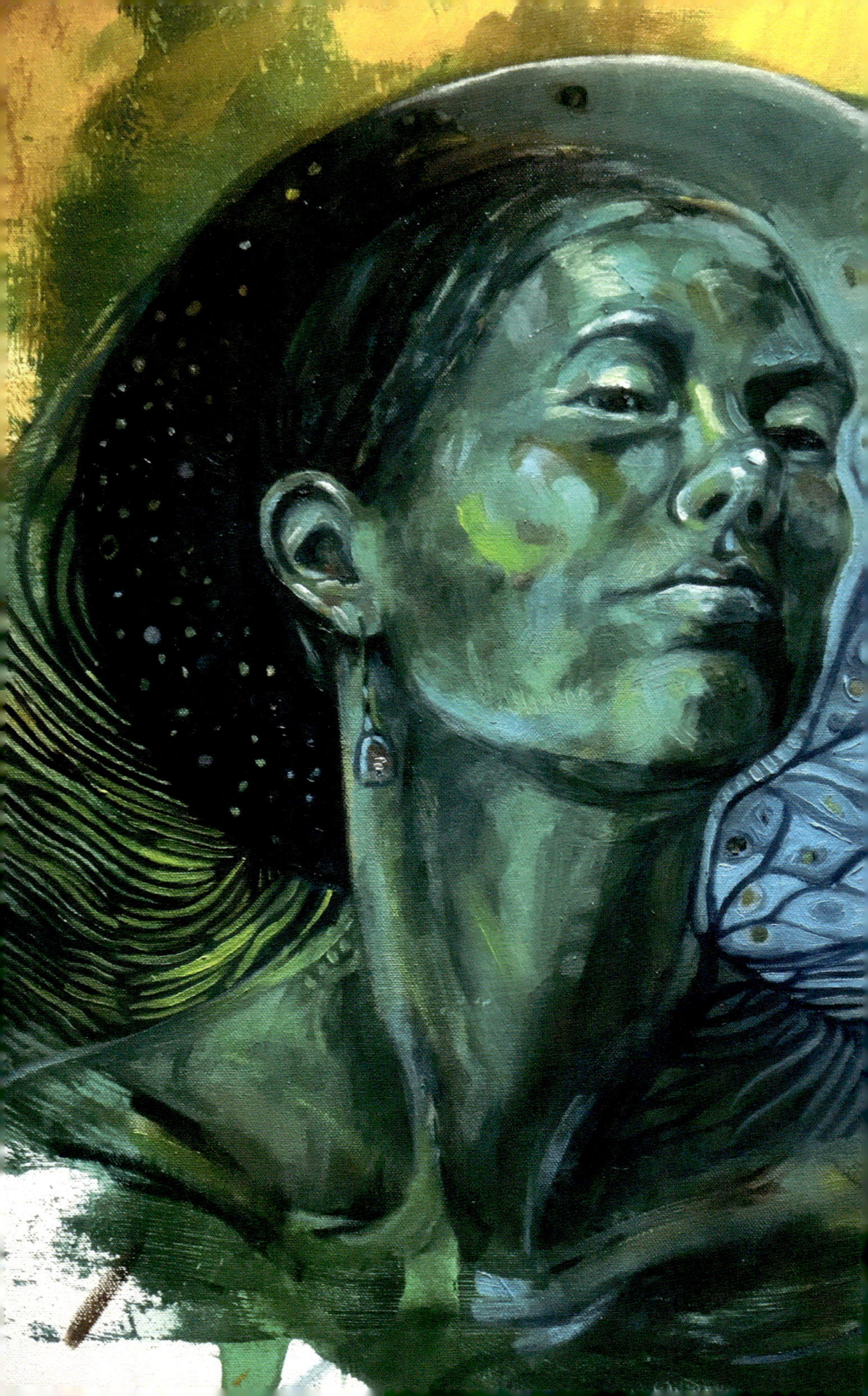

Transition

Sometimes there is an ease in change
a knowing, an awe
that this is not just necessary
but with the unseen power of a moon's
gravitational strength pulling the tide
we are drawn forward

A knowing
an intelligence of what to do
without question
a bird's song at dawn
they just know their voice is needed
to sing the world awake

In autumn leaves just fall
trees trust transition
it is not a choice
but a wisdom of phases
a continual and joyous
tuning into of purpose
to become exactly as you are
to arrive crossing this threshold
triumphant

AFFIRMATION

I move from the place of my inner-knowing and deepest desires
I trust my decision to make this necessary change, divinely guided
I courageously embark on this transition to support my becoming

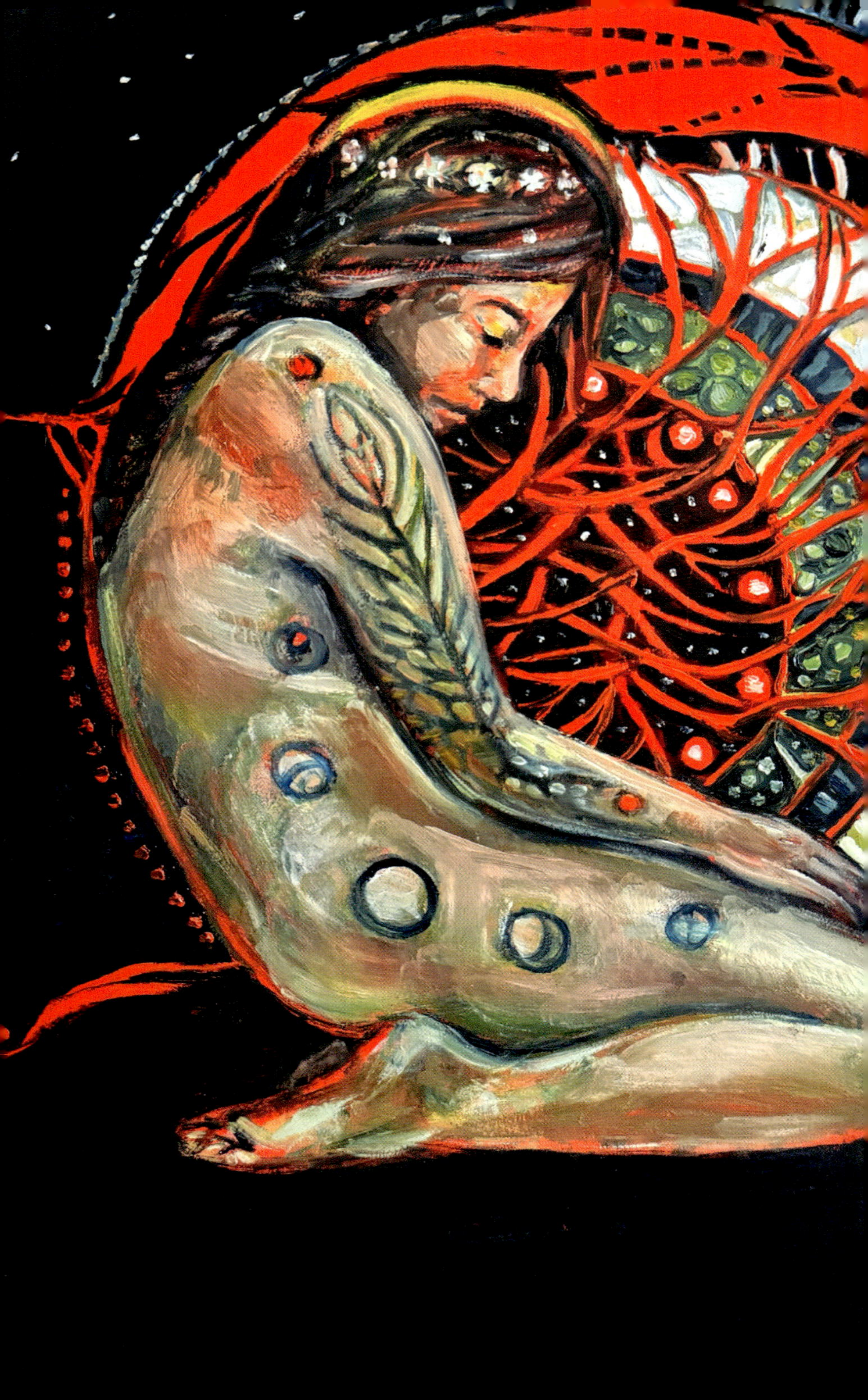

Treasure

Healing isn't an erasure

It is the kneeling down in a gravel pit
of everything you've been given
and finding every last bright underbelly
of rough edged rock
turned over
the orange and white flames of
the agate that formed
burning, burning
somehow smooth, shiny
soft to the touch

Healing is a miracle
from a crevice, a cavity, a breaking open
from the volcanic eruptions of living
in these holes there is a magic
of mineral, water, and oxygen all spinning
from seemingly nothing
a void
alchemizing, pouring out quartz
and gorgeous multicolored gems
the crystallization of what was, what was
pooling, settling in reverence, to stillness
into the beauty of who you are now
and that protective shell
it softens, softens
eventually fades
revealing the treasure
you have become

AFFIRMATION

I trust in the alchemy of my healing and the innate wisdom of my body
I now see the miraculous ways wounds do not have to break us,
but can break us open
I honor the treasure I have become through it all

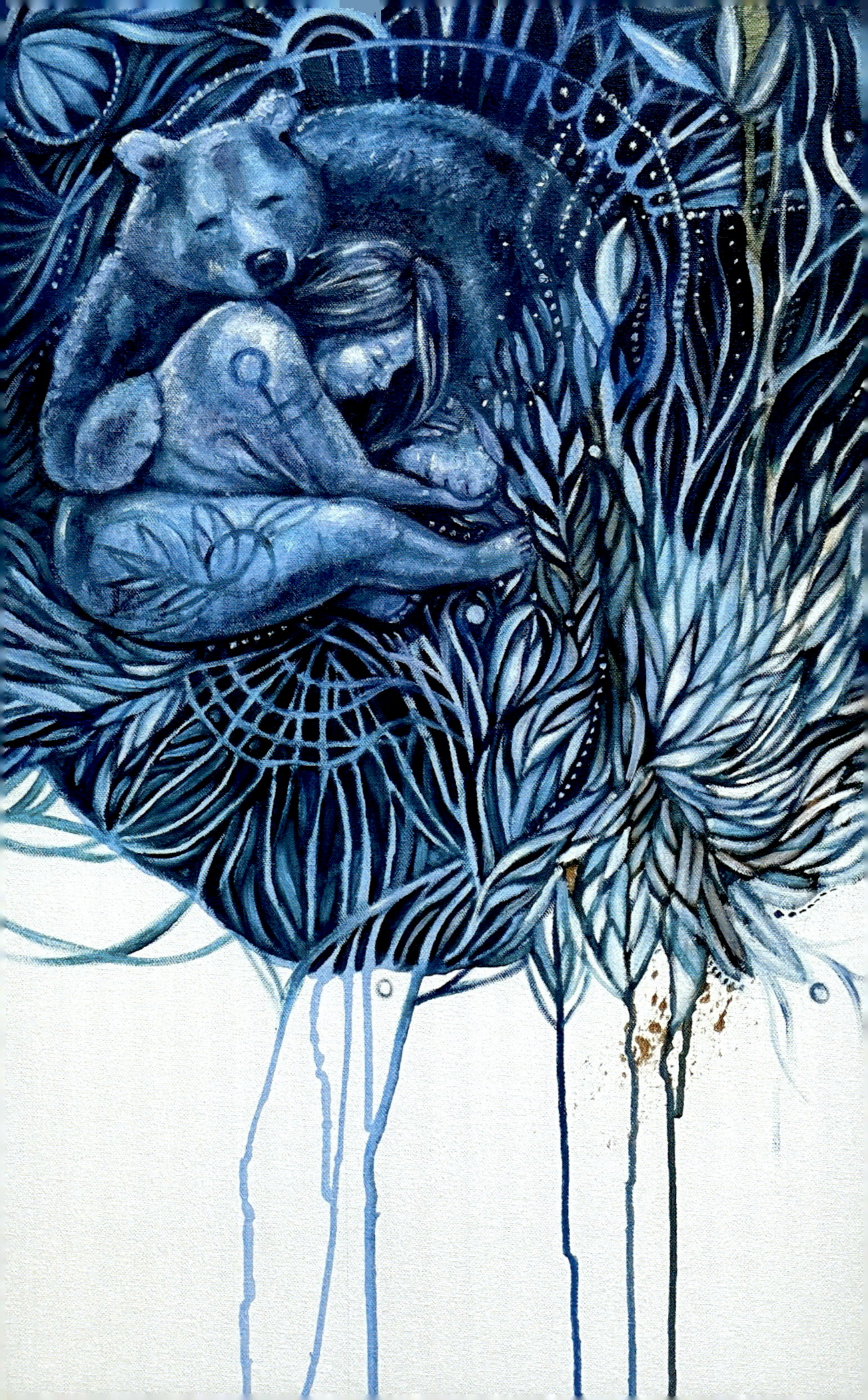

Untangling the Voices

They are guides within, my parts, mesmerized and terrorized by my life. Speak me into existence through my lifespan. Their voices a spindrift, propelling me along my perpetual becoming.

And this is all of me, my wholeness. Every part carries their own pearl of wisdom, shining opalescent. Their heart beats only for me, wrapped in a womb of their own universe. Constellations across the galaxy of my being. Each wants to be known, heard, seen. There are burdens they carry and ways only they walk that light up the forest floor within me. Each footstep bursting with the magic needed to awaken me.

All the voices call out to me in their own ways. Sometimes they shout, take the wheel, swerve. Often I get lost in their tangle.

The wise ones have said we are the great "I Am." I was I, thou was thou, there is nothing I am not, *the splendor of recognition*.

I know I hold the power of the Great Black Bear. Protector, comforter, lifter of heavy things only I can soothe. Untangle the voices from their ratty braid, brush through the snarls until smooth. Gently stroke their foreheads and teach them the ancient lullabies, until they are a chorus within. And I the conductor can only create the music of my Life. Urging each voice to sing in the way only they were born to.

AFFIRMATION

I connect with my Self energy and reclaim my core, undamaged essence
I listen and tend lovingly to all the parts of myself that long to be known and held
I am inherently wise, compassionate, and capable of healing
I create the safety, support, and space needed to awaken my unique medicine

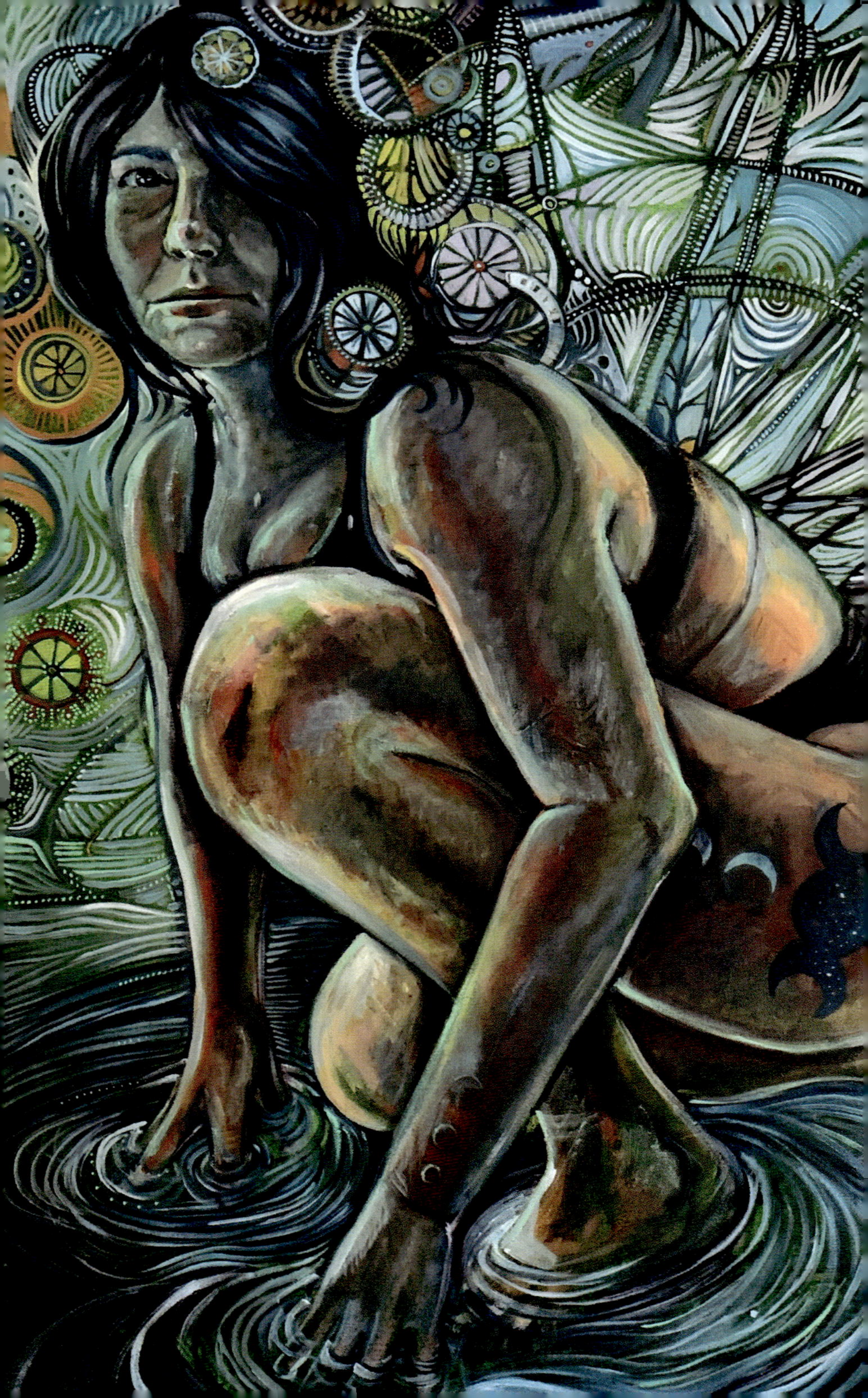

Walk Across Water

Lake Superior collides with winter, adjusts and inhales,
holding herself steady within the season's frozen offering.

Suspended for this moment. Changing form with the ever
changing world, freezing in the places that make contact
with what is before her, the armor needed to endure.

We can exist like this too, gathering ourselves amidst
the sometimes cold shoreline of circumstance,
the rough edges of our lives.

Whatever we are up against, we can find the shape
of our being expanding, shifting, transforming.

Isn't this a miracle, the ice only ever once
exactly like today.

These brilliant small white rugged sculptures
mountains of glowing ice and smooth stone colored
valleys against a striking blue horizon
fierce brushstrokes of pink wisped above
filled with smoke signals,
these floating steamy clouds.

See now how we can walk across the water like never before,
so close, can almost touch the sky.

AFFIRMATION

I have the capacity to shift and transform through anything I am up against
I appreciate the miraculous ways I adapt to endure life's challenges
I honor the unique beauty in how I have grown through adversity

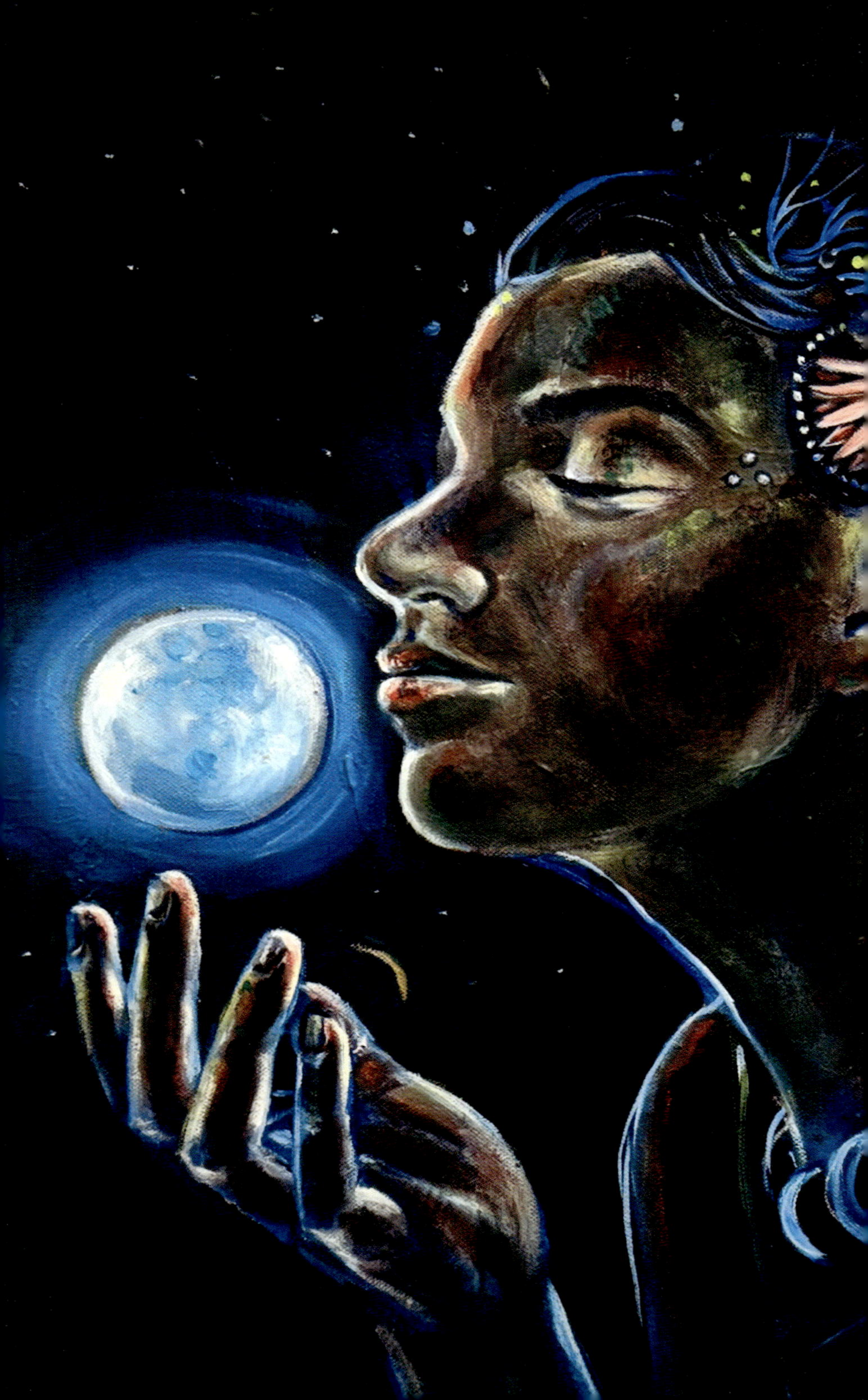

What Was

Suspended beyond space and time
in soft folds of memories
delicate as silk
we can run our fingers along
what was
whenever we like
(remembering, cherishing)

AFFIRMATION

I hold steady in the present moment
I move with grace amidst the ever-changing tides of life
I know all the love and beauty I've experienced
is mine to cherish and hold for always

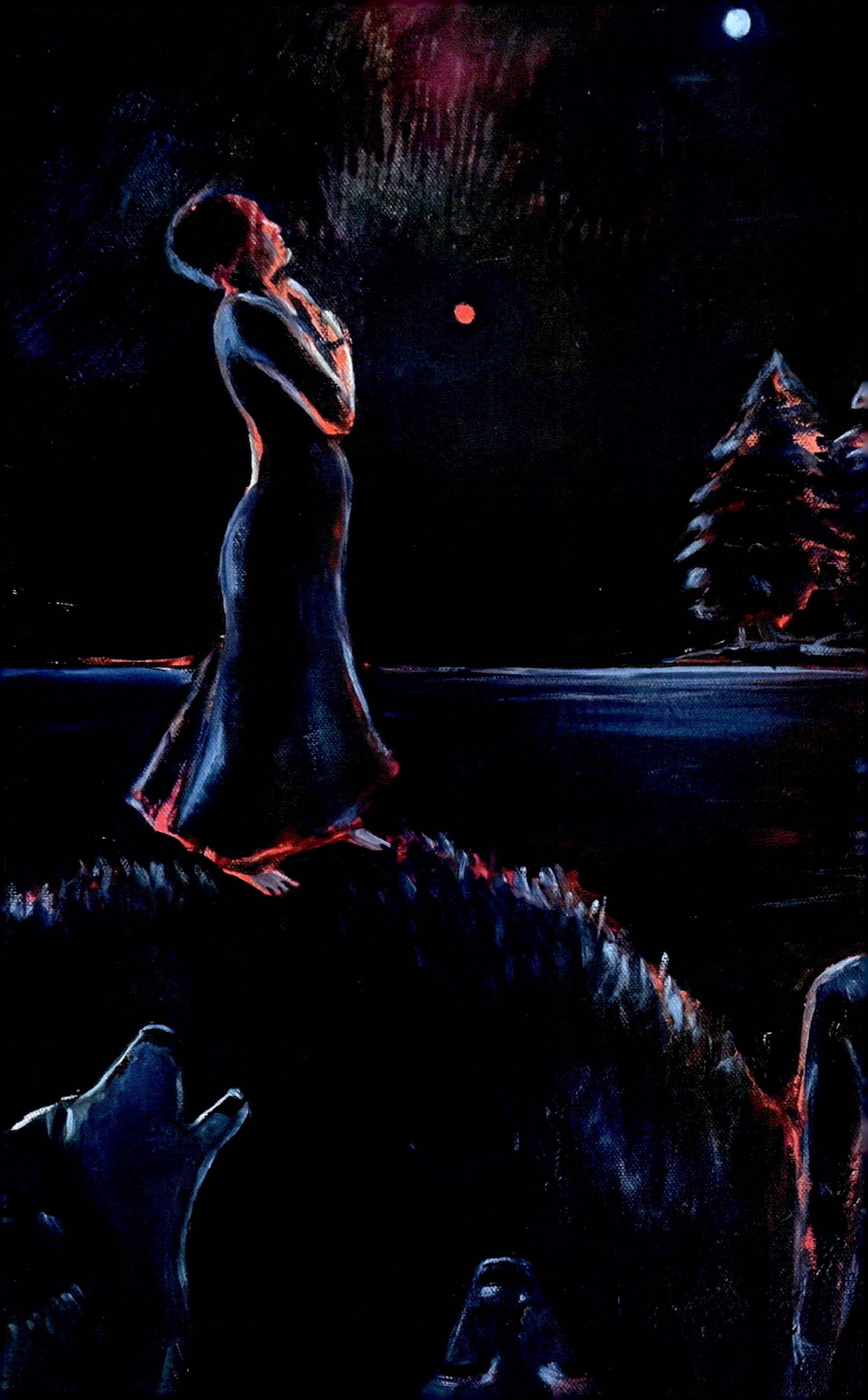

Wolves

With this darkness setting in
I watch as a full moon rises
appreciating every miraculous shade
of light it captures
brilliant pink with fire orange heart
at the horizon, lifting up fierce yellow
as the eyes of a great horned owl
at its highest point
gleaming white
as the teeth of a momma bear

Like wolves, I just howl
the only thing I know to do, I howl
and howl, and howl
and my pack howls with me

I am not alone
this primal chorus carries me forward
this moonlight illuminates my way
into the night
opening up before me

AFFIRMATION

I am never alone, no matter the darkness
I am held by my community, my wolf-pack
I have the resources to support me
and illuminate my way forward

PAINTING INDEX

Sarah Brokke's paintings as they appear are cropped from their original format and are listed below by page number. Many of the original works are held in private collections.

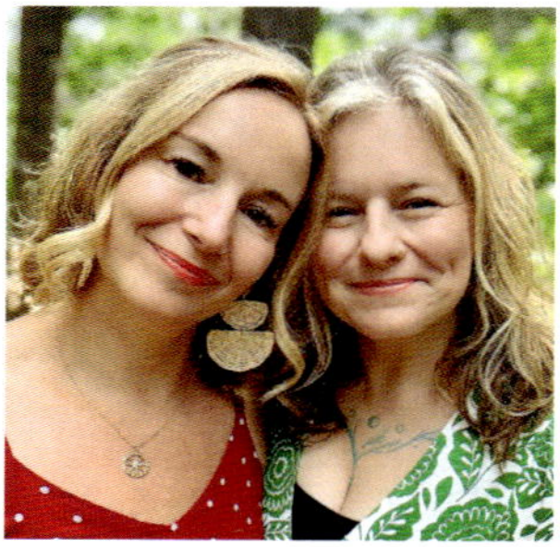

Kyle Leia Heyesen *(left)* is a mother, wife, social worker, writer, mystical poetess, trauma-conscious teacher, yoga guide, and visionary. She writes as a means to process life, both the difficult to bear and the beautifully sacred and awe-inspiring. Her intention is to create a life and world that embodies mindfulness, compassion, reverence, and awakened consciousness. She believes that through our healing, often supported with gifts from transformational offerings such as poetry, art, music, and yoga, we experience greater personal and collective wholeness and belonging.

Find her at kyleleia.com

Sarah Brokke *(right)* is a painter, illustrator, muralist, retreat guide, and is an Associate Professor of Art. She received her BFA from the University of Minnesota Duluth. She earned her MFA through a joint program between SACI in Florence, Italy and Bowling Green State University. Brokke has exhibited nationally and internationally, and continues to make work today focused on the intersection between nature and humanity, and seeking the sacred in all beings.

Find more of her work at sarahbrokke.com

ACKNOWLEDGEMENTS

Thank you to Deb Davidsavor, our dear friend and graphic designer for her brilliant creativity, support, consultation, guidance, and incredible talent. To Angie Mason, our steadfast editor, for her keen eye, clear feedback, and compassionate input. To Sam Connolly for her support, editing extraordinaire, consultation, and feedback. You have both made our body of work stronger and more essential. To Rebecca James Alsum at Svälja Whole-Being for her love and support of our project, hosting our Irrevocable Wholeness exhibit, micro-retreat, and book release party at the studio. Endless gratitude! Rhonda Awsumb at Pro-Print for your expertise, support, and partnership creating our book and oracle cards. Deep bows of gratitude to our families, our friends who have become our families and our beloved community; we could not create our work without your love and support. Reverence to the beautiful land we live on and with, near the shores of Lake Superior.

This work is made possible in part by the voters of Minnesota through a grant from the Arrowhead Regional Arts Council, thanks to a legislative appropriation from the arts and cultural heritage fund. And by Kickstarter, a funding platform for creative projects, which allowed our family, friends and supportive community members to back this project financially — thank you!